Meaning and

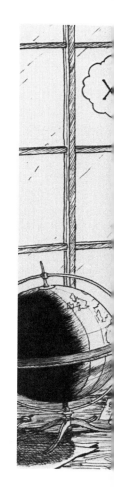

Meaning and Mental Representation

Robert Cummins

A Bradford Book
The MIT Press
Cambridge, Massachusetts
London, England

This book was set in Palatino and was printed and bound by
Halliday Lithograph in the United States of America.

Library of Congress Cataloging in Publication Data

Cummins, Robert.
    Meaning and mental representation/ Robert Cummins.
    p.   cm.
    "A Bradford book."
    Includes index.
    ISBN 0-262-03139-6
    1. Representation (Philosophy) 2. Mind and body 3. Knowledge, Theory
    of. 4. Meaning. 5. Science — Philosophy. I. Title.
B105.R4C86 1988   88-856
153— dc19   CIP

Philosophy of science is philosophy enough.

W. V. O. Quine

Contents

Acknowledgments

Many students and colleagues have helped make this a better book than it would have been had I been left to my own devices. I would like especially to thank Georg Schwarz, Paul Smolensky, Georges Rey, David Kirsh, and Ned Block. My greatest debt is to Denise Dellarosa Cummins, who, through constant example and constructive criticism, prevented me from drifting into philosophical disputes that have lost touch with the practice of empirical research and explanation in cognitive science. The art work is by Brian Orr.

Meaning and Mental Representation

Chapter 1
Identifying the Problem and Other Preliminaries

Two Problems about Representation

We should be careful to distinguish two problems about mental representation. The first—the Problem of Representations (plural)—is a theoretical problem in empirical science. Although we know that states of and processes in the nervous system play the role of representations in biological systems, it is an open question just which states and processes are involved in which activities, and how. Moreover, it is an open question how these states or processes should be characterized. For example, orthodox computationalism holds that mental representations are realized as symbolic data structures, but there is considerable controversy among orthodox computationalists as to what kinds of data structures are involved in various processes. Connectionists (see, e.g., Rumelhart et al. 1986), on the other hand, hold that mental representations are realized as activation levels of ensembles of simple processors, and/or as the strengths of the connections among such processors. The problem to which these approaches offer competing responses is that of discovering a way of characterizing representations that will allow us to understand both their physical instantiations and their systematic roles in mental processes.

The second problem—the Problem of *Representation* (singular) —is, at least as I understand it, a paradigmatic problem in the philosophy of science. To a large extent, empirical theories of cognition can and do take the notion of mental content as an explanatory primitive. But this is a kind of explanatory loan

(Dennett 1978): If it turns out that the notion of mental representation cannot be given a satisfactory explication— if, in particular, no account of the nature of the (mental) representation relation can be given that is consistent with the empirical theory that assumes it—then, at least in this respect, that empirical theory must be regarded as ill founded, and hence as a less than adequate response to the drive for the kind of thorough intellectual understanding that motivates scientific theory in the first place.

We can get a better idea of what these two problems are, and how they are related, by surveying in very general terms the various answers that have been tendered to each of them.

The Problem of Representations

It is surprising that only four answers have been suggested concerning the sorts of things that can be mental representations. I am not certain that this list of ours is exhaustive, but every proposal I know of fits pretty clearly into one of these four. It doesn't really matter much; my topic is the nature of representation, not what sorts of things do the representational work of the mind. I survey the alternatives here mainly to help to put the main problem in some context.

Mind-stuff inFORMed   An important scholastic theory holds that in perception the immaterial mind becomes inFORMed by the same FORMS that inFORM the thing perceived. The background metaphysics assumes that knowable or perceivable things are a combination of matter and FORM: the *stuff* and its properties. There are two basically different kinds of *stuff:* mental stuff and physical stuff. When physical stuff is inFORMed by redness and sphericity, the result is a physical red ball. When mental stuff is inFORMed by redness and sphericity, the result is an idea of a red ball—or, perhaps better, the result is a red ball *as mental object* (i.e., as idea) rather than a red ball *as material object*. According to this theory, when you perceive a red ball, the very same FORMS that make the physical object of your perception red and spherical make your idea red and spherical. But of course a red ball *in*

Figure 1.1
Aristotle mentally representing Graycat with a ball.

idea is a very different thing than red ball *in matter*. A red ball *in idea* doesn't take up physical space, though it does take up *mental* space.

The basic idea behind this theory is that to know something is, in a pretty straightforward sense, to *be* it. You know the red ball when you see it because *you* have what *it* has: redness and sphericity. Your mind literally *is* just what the physical stuff is, because to *be* red and spherical is just to be inFORMed by redness and sphericity. This doctrine seems to make the notion of mental representation perfectly transparent: The idea represents the red ball, and it represents it as red and as spherical because the idea *is* red and spherical and the redness and sphericity come from the physical ball. To represent the world is to have a model of it in (on?) your mind—a model made of different stuff, as models usually are, but a model just the same. It we draw a picture, we, as theorists, can just *see* what represents what—e.g., the thing on the left part of the thought represents the cat, and the thing on the right part of the thought represents the ball. According to this theory, representation is evidently founded on similarity (shared properties)—a similarity the theorist can just *see*. Of course, the thinker can't just see it, as Berkeley and Hume eventually pointed out, but that is an epistemological problem at most. The fact that we can't see the alleged similarity between our own mental representations and what they represent (or see the representations at all, for that matter) doesn't show that it isn't similarity that underwrites representation; it only emphasizes the trivial fact that we can't hope to infer the way the world is from prior knowledge of the fact that we have it represented correctly.

Images   The favorite theory of Berkeley and Hume was that mental representations are images. Except for dropping the Aristotelian jargon, however, this is just the same theory over again; the "picture" in both cases is just the same. Images were frequently said to be red and spherical, though with some uneasiness. The scholastic metaphysics was gone, but the basic idea was the same: Images represent things in virtue of resembling them—i.e., in virtue of sharing properties with them (though, of course, a sphere in the mind—i.e., as it exists as an image—takes up no

Figure 1.2
Berkeley's mental representations look just like Aristotle's.

physical space, only mental space; it occupies a portion of the visual field, for example).

Symbols   Haugeland (1985) credits Hobbes with being the first to have an inkling that mental representations might be language-like symbols. This is now the orthodox position, insofar as there is such a thing. The main thing to realize at this stage is just that if mental representations are symbols, then mental representation cannot be founded on similarity; symbols don't resemble the things they represent. The great advantage of symbols as representations is that they can be the inputs and outputs of *computations*. Putting these two things together gives us a quick account of the possibility of thought about abstractions. When you calculate, you think about numbers by manipulating symbols. The symbols don't resemble the numbers, of course (what would resemble a number?), but they are readily manipulated.

Connectionists also hold that mental representations are symbols, but they deny that these symbols are data structures (i.e., objects of computation). In orthodox computational theory the objects of computation are identical with the objects of semantic interpretation, but in connectionist models (at least in those using truly distributed representation) this is not the case.[1] Connectionists also typically deny that mental symbols are language-like. This is not surprising; given that the symbols are not the objects of computation, there would be no obvious way to exploit a language-like syntactic structure in the symbols anyway.

(Actual) neurophysiological states   The crucial claim here is that mental representations cannot be identified at any level more abstract than actual neurophysiology. Mental representation, on this view, is a biological phenomenon essentially. Mental representations cannot be realized in, say, a digital computer, no matter how "brain-like" its architecture happens to be at some nonbiological level of description.

Like symbols, neurophysiological states cannot represent things in virtue of resembling them. Advocates of symbols or neurophysiological states must ground representation in something other than similarity.

FRAME: GRAYCAT
KIND OF: CAT
HABITS:
    OVEREATS
    OVERSLEEPS
    CHASES MICE
PROPERTIES:
    COLOR: GRAY
    SMART
    KNEW HOBBES
    SELFISH
    HAS BELIEFS,
        AND DESIRES

Figure 1.3
Hobbes representing Graycat.

Figure 1.4
Hebb mentally representing Graycat.

The Problem of Representation

More surprising than the dearth of candidates to play the role of mental representations is the dearth of suggestions concerning the nature of representation itself. There are, I think, only four: similarity, covariance, adaptational role, and functional role. Each of these will be the subject of a chapter. For now, I will supply only brief intuitive sketches.

Similarity   The thought that representation is grounded in similarity is what drives the idea that mental representations are in-FORMed mind stuff, or images. The crucial intuition, I think, is this: If you are going to think about things in the world, you need something to go proxy for those things in thought. You cannot, of course, literally turn over cats or the body politic in your mind; all you can turn over is ideas. But this, it seems, will be no help unless ideas are *like* the cats or the body politic: How could having an idea of a cat help you know about cats unless the idea is like the cat? I could say, "OK, this salt shaker represents the pitcher, and the pepper shaker represents the batter." But wouldn't *pictures* be much better—especially moving pictures, such as those in Rod Carew's batting instruction video?

Covariance   The idea that representation is grounded in covariance or causation is most naturally motivated by reflecting on vision research.[2] How do we decide, for example, that a certain neural structure in the visual cortex of a frog is a motion detector? Roughly, we notice that a certain characteristic activity in the structure covaries with the presence of moving objects in the frog's field of vision. Given this fact, it seems natural to suppose that what *makes* that structure a motion detector is just the fact that it fires when there is motion in the frog's field of vision. What else could it be? So the fact that the firing of the structure in question represents the occurrence of motion in the frog's visual field is just constituted by the covariance between the firings and the motions represented. If you are attracted to covariance theories, you aren't going to think much of the idea that representations are images, because the similarities images promise to deliver are going to be irrelevant.

Adaptational role   The idea that representation is grounded in adaptational role is most easily understood as a reaction to certain problems facing covariance theories. The orientation of a bee dance represents the location of flowers to spectator bees, but it doesn't covary with the location of flowers any better than it covaries with lots of things it doesn't represent, e.g., the absence of an insecticide cloud in the indicated direction. Millikan (1984) points out that we take "flowers over there" to be the content of the dance, even if flowers are not often "over there" (and hence there is no substantial covariance), because the cases in which spectators have found flowers (hence food) "over there" account for the continued replication of the dance and the characteristic response it evokes in spectators.

Functional or computational role   This is just functionalism applied to mental representations. Functionalism says that a mental state is what it is in virtue of its functional role. It is functional roles that individuate mental states. But mental representations are, by definition, individuated by their contents. Hence, content must depend on functional role.[3]

Meanings and Meaningfulness

When we ask what it is in virtue of which something (a mental state, a stop sign, a linguistic utterance) has a meaning or has semantic content, there are two quite different things we may have in mind. We may be asking what it is in virtue of which things of the sort in question have any meaning at all, or we may be asking what it is in virtue of which some particular thing or type of thing has some particular meaning. Although it is rather obvious that a theory that answers the first sort of question (a theory of meaningfulness) needn't provide answers to question of the second sort, it is not so obvious that a theory that provides answers to questions of the second sort (a theory of meaning) must also be a theory of meaningfulness. All the theories I will examine in this book are intended primarily as theories of meaning, not as theories of meaningfulness; but each of them entails, in an obvious way, a theory of meaningfulness. I shall try to make this explicit and, when appropriate, to be clear about whether the theory is being expressed and evaluated as a theory of meaning or as a theory of meaningfulness.

Theories of meaning, in the sense just staked out, should be sharply distinguished from theories that, as it were, distribute meanings (or some other semantic property) over the things that have them. For example, it is perfectly possible to articulate a theory that specifies a truth condition for every sentence in a language but that is entirely neutral concerning what it is in virtue of which a sentence has any truth condition at all, or in virtue of which it has the particular truth condition it happens to have. Tarski's theory of truth is, notoriously, just such a theory— truth is defined in terms of satisfaction, and satisfaction is defined recursively. The theory is completely silent about what satisfaction is. If we ask "In virtue of what is 'X$_1$ is a cat' satisfied by every sequence beginning with a cat?" the theory gives no answer (see Field 1971 and Cummins 1975a). Linguists and psychologists want to know which things have which meanings, and why. Philosophers want to know what it is to have a meaning. With any luck, good philosophy might help with the "why" part of the question asked by linguists and psychologists. By my lights, that is really the only thing that could make it good philosophy.[4]

"Content"

When we suppose a system to harbor cognitive representations, we are supposing that the system harbors states, or perhaps even objects, that are semantically individuated. Thus, the central question about mental representation is this: What is it for a mental state to have a semantic property? Equivalently, what makes a state (or an object) in a cognitive system a *representation?*

When we ask what it is for a cognitive state to have a semantic property, there are a number of different things on which we might choose to focus. What is it for a cognitive state to have a truth condition? What is it for a cognitive state to be about something, or to refer to something, or to be true of something?[5] What is it for a cognitive state to be an intentional state (i.e., to have intentional properties)? The (very) recent tendency in philosophy has been to see all these questions as depending on two prior questions: What is it for a cognitive state to have a content? What is it for such a state to have some specified content, e.g., the content *that Brutus had flat feet* or the content *square?* This, I think, is a useful way to proceed—not because the notion of content is especially clear or simple, but because "content" can function in philosophical investigation as a kind of generic term for whatever it is that underwrites semantic and intentional properties generally. There is little to be gained, and there is a non-negligible risk of bias, if we begin by focusing in a fussy way on semantic or intentional concepts borrowed from theoretical or common-sense discourse about language and the attitudes— concepts that may not apply in any straightforward way to the problem of characterizing the representations assumed by con- temporary cognitive theory. In what follows, when I write of the semantics of cognitive systems, or of representations, I mean to address these still poorly defined questions of "content." Since I shall be examining various "theories of content," there is no point in trying to say in advance what "content" means; let the theories speak for themselves. Meanwhile, our intuitive grasp of the thing will have to do.

Methodology

It is commonplace for philosophers to address the question of mental representation in abstraction from any particular scientific theory or theoretical framework. I regard this as a mistake. Mental representation is a theoretical assumption, not a com- monplace of ordinary discourse. To suppose that "common- sense psychology" ("folk psychology"), orthodox computation- alism, connectionism, neuroscience, and so on all make use of the same notion of representation seems naive. Moreover, to under- stand the notion of mental representation that grounds some particular theoretical framework, one must understand the ex- planatory role that framework assigns to mental representation. It is precisely because mental representation has different ex- planatory roles in "folk psychology," orthodox computationalism, connectionism, and neuroscience that it is naive to suppose that each makes use of the same notion of mental representation. We must not, then, ask simply (and naively) "What is the nature of mental representation?"; this is a hopelessly unconstrained question. Instead, we must pick a theoretical framework and ask what explanatory role mental representation plays in that framework and what the representation relation must be if that explanatory role is to be well grounded. Our question should be "What must we suppose about the nature of mental representation if orthodox computational theories (or connectionist theories, or whatever) of cognition are to turn out to be true and explanatory?" As I understand this question, it is a question in the philosophy of science exactly analogous to the following question in the philosophy of physics: What must we suppose the nature of space to be (substance? property? relation?) if General Relativity is to turn out to be true and explanatory?

The bulk of this book is an attempt to evaluate existing accounts of the nature of mental representation in the context of computational theories of cognition. By computational theories of cognition I mean *orthodox* computational theories—theories that assume that cognitive systems are automatic interpreted formal systems in the sense of Haugeland (1981, 1985), i.e., that cognition is disciplined symbol manipulation.[6] In the final chapter, I will consider briefly how things might look in a connectionist context.

Computational theories assume that mental representations are symbolic data structures as these are understood in computer science. This is the computationalist answer to the Problem of *Representations*. Although the instantiation of symbolic data structures in the brain is problematic, orthodox computationalism has demonstrated the physical instantiability of such structures and has made considerable progress toward demonstrating that at least some cognitive processes can be understood as symbol manipulation. But, like all theoretical frameworks in cognitive science, orthodox computationalism is silent about the nature of representation itself; it is entirely agnostic concerning what it is for a data structure to have semantic properties. Nevertheless, certain possibilities are ruled out by the empirical assumptions of the theory, as we will see.

I will need a short, convenient way to refer to what I have been calling orthodox computationalism; I'll call it the CTC, for the computational theory of cognition.

Representation and Intentionality

This preliminary issue of the explanatory role of mental representation in some particular theoretical framework would not be troubling if mental representation were a *commonplace* rather than a (variously) theoretically motivated *hypothesis*. Most philosophers aren't troubled; they think mental representation *is* a commonplace. They think this because they assume that the problem of mental representation is just the problem of intentionality—i.e., that representational content is intentional content. As I use the term, a system with intentionality is just a system with ordinary propositional attitudes (belief, desire, and so on). Thus construed, intentionality is a commonplace, and hence so is intentional content. So the assumption I want to scout is the assumption that the problem of mental representation is just the problem of what attaches beliefs and desires to their contents.[7]

Although it is evidently a mistake to identify intentionality with representation, there is a widely bruited philosophical theory, mainly due to Fodor, that forges a close connection between intentional contents and representational contents. I call this theory the *representational theory of intentionality* (RTI). The RTI holds that intentional states inherit their contents from representations that are their constituents. The familiar ur-theory goes like this: To have a belief is to have a representation in one's belief box—a box distinguished from the desire box by its function, i.e., by which processes can put things in and take things out. (Belief-box contents are available as premises in inference; desire-box contents are available as goals, i.e., conditions whose satisfaction ends processing cycles.) My belief that U.S. policy in Central America is folly is *about* Central America because the relevant representation in my belief box represents Central America.[8] The RTI has some nice features. Most notably, it captures the two attributes of the propositional attitudes to which we allude when we call them by that name: that they have propositional contents and that believing involves taking a different "attitude" toward a proposition than desiring. But in spite of its nice features, the RTI is no truism; it is a controversial and powerful empirical theory.

If you accept the RTI explicitly, you will, of course, want a theory of mental representation that attaches intentional contents—the contents of propositional attitudes—to representational states. You will also want a theory of mental representation like this if you are merely sloppy about the difference between mental representation and the attitudes. I think this particular bit of sloppiness is pretty common in a lot of recent philosophical discussion of mental representation, but it doesn't really matter; anyone who assumes, for whatever reason, that a theory of mental representation must give us intentional contents (e.g., objects of belief) is making a very large assumption, an assumption that isn't motivated by an examination of the role representation plays in any current empirical theories. After all, it isn't belief of any stripe that most theoretical appeals to mental representation are designed to capture. Just think of psycholinguistics, which got all this representation talk started. The data structures of your favorite parser are not even *prima facie* candidates for belief contents. This is nonaccidentally related to the fact that the CTC, as we will see in chapter 8, makes use of a notion of representation that is at home in computational systems generally, not just in cognitive systems and certainly not just in intentional systems. If we begin our investigation of mental representation by focusing on intentional states, we will miss what is most distinctive about representation as invoked by the CTC. We certainly do not want to assume, therefore, that the contents of beliefs as ordinarily attributed are the contents of any representations in a computational system. We need to keep open the possibility that, e.g., belief attribution, though a legitimate case of semantic characterization, is not a semantic characterization of any representation in the believer (Dennett 1978; Stalnaker 1984; Cummins 1987).

The fact that current philosophers who are interested in mental representation do not follow the methodological path that I recommended in the last section is explained to some extent by the prevalence of the assumption (often bolstered by the RTI) that the problem of mental representation is to explain how intentional contents (the contents of belief, desire, etc.) get attached to mental states. This assumption puts very strong constraints on the theory of mental representation. In fact, the constraints are so strong—so hard to satisfy—that one is never tempted to look elsewhere for something to constrain the problem; the last thing one needs is another constraint. Thus, you will never be moved to ask after such things as the explanatory role of representation in, say, John Anderson's ACT* (1983). Conversely, once you abandon (or at least question) the idea that the theory of mental representation must yield contents for intentional states, you *need* a few constraints, and the explanatory structure of a theory that invokes the notion of representation is the natural place to look.

Inexplicit Content [9]

The attribution of intentional states (beliefs and desires) is not the only kind of semantic characterization of cognitive systems that must be distinguished from explanatory appeals to representational states. A computational system can also be semantically characterized in virtue of features of its structure. Here are some examples.

Content implicit in the state of control   A word processor's search routine tries to match the character currently being read against the second character of the target only if the character read last matched the first character of the target. If it is now trying to match the second character, the current state of control carries the information that the first character matched the last character read; however, the system creates no data structure with this content. Nowhere is that information explicitly represented.

Content implicit in the domain   I give you instructions for getting to my house from yours, all in such terms as "go left after three intersections" and "turn right at the first stop sign after the barn." Perhaps I even include things like "Make a left down the alley with the blue Chevy van parked in it," because I know you will be coming after 5 o'clock and I know that the van is always parked there after that time. I rely on this in the same way I rely on the barn's staying put. Now, if you (or anything else) execute this program, you will get to my house. In the process, you never create a representation of the form "Cummins lives at location L"; yet, given the terrain, a system executing this program does "know where Cummins lives."

Content implicit in the form of representation   Most of us don't know how to multiply (or even add) roman numerals. "XXII times LXIV" has the same *meaning* as "22 times 64," but the partial-products algorithm we all learned in school exploits information that is implicit in the second *form* but not present in the first—e.g., that shifting a column to the left amounts to multiplying by 10. This is the famous problem of knowledge representation in artificial intelligence: find a form that makes more efficient or psychologically realistic algorithms possible.

Content implicit in the medium of representation   Are the two parts of figure 1.5 the same? If you had each one on a transparency, you could simply put one over the other and rotate them relative to each other to see if they would match. But this works only because of two properties of the *medium* (i.e., the transparencies): They are transparent, and they are rigid in the plane of the figures. When you rotate them, the information about the relative spatial relations of parts of a figure to other parts is implicit in the medium; its rigidity carries the information that these relations remain constant. A different medium might not carry this information, and you would then have to represent it explicitly.

I am sure these examples don't exhaust the cases in which content can be attributed to a computational system in the absence of any explicit representation having the content in question. I have listed them here only to emphasize the fact that represented content isn't all the content there is. There is also inexplicit content of various kinds, and if nothing like the RTI is true there is also intentional content.[10]

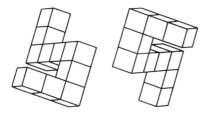

Figure 1.5
Are these the same figure?

Representation and the Language of Thought

Representation is often identified with what is really only one kind of representation: quasi-linguistic representation of the sort featured in Fodor's book *The Language of Thought* (1975). But it is at least possible that cognitive states might involve representations of some sort without involving quasi-linguistic formulas type-identified by their status in an internal code with a recursive syntax. In this book, when I mean language-like representations—sentences, or their constituents, written in a brain or in some other physical medium—I will make that explicit. In this connection, it is important to keep in mind that representations may well have propositional contents even though those representations are not language-like, for I take it that an essential feature of the Language-of-Thought Hypothesis—the hypothesis that mental representations are language-like—is that mental representations have a syntax comparable to that of a natural or an artificial language. But it is perfectly obvious that a symbol can have a propositional content—can have a proposition as its proper interpretation—even though it has no syntax and is not part of a language-like system of symbols. Paul Revere's lanterns are a simple case in point.

Cognition and the Mental

As is no doubt obvious by now, the use of the word "mental" in the title is misleading, for I will be talking about cognitive systems rather than minds. Some cognitive systems are not

minds (not, at least, as we know minds ostensively), and many aspects of mentality are not cognitive. Cognitive science is founded on the empirical assumption that cognition (hence the study of cognitive systems) is a natural and relatively autonomous domain of inquiry. I shall simply accept this assumption, but a few brief comments are in order.

When we run through mental phenomena as we know them from the human case, many seem inessential in that something could be a mind without exhibiting them. For example, it seems plausible to suppose that a creature could have a mind without having emotions, as is supposed to be the case with Star Trek's Mr. Spock. Descartes held that the essence of mind is thought, Locke that it is the capacity for thought. A system that could do nothing but think might be a rather colorless mind by human standards, but there seems to be something to the traditional idea that such a system would nevertheless *be* a mind. On the other hand, a system that could not think but could feel, have emotions, and so on does not seem to qualify as a mind. If this is right, then what cognitive science proposes is not, after all, very novel; it is just the idea that thinking (and/or the capacity for thought) is the essence of mind and can be studied independently of other mental phenomena.

It is important to be clear about what this hypothesis does and does not accomplish in the way of creating scientific elbow room. It *does* make it possible for the cognitive scientist to ignore (provisionally, at least) such mental phenomena as moods, emotions, sensations, and—most important—consciousness. The hypothesis that cognition is a relatively autonomous domain does not, however, entitle the cognitive scientist to ignore either human psychology or neuroscience. Human beings are the best and only uncontroversial example of cognitive systems we have to study. To try to study cognition without paying attention to how humans cognize would be like trying to study genetics without bothering about biochemistry; some progress is possible, but not a great deal.

Most objections to materialist theories of mind proceed by trying to establish either that a purely physical system could not

be a cognitive system or that a purely physical system could not be conscious. A materialist theory of *cognition* requires a response to the first sort of argument. But materialists, protected by the empirical hypothesis that cognition is separable from mentality generally, can afford to put off responding to the charge that a purely physical system could not be conscious. Perhaps consciousness isn't essential to mind in the way that cognition is.[11] This does not make the problem of consciousness go away, but it does make it, provisionally, someone else's problem.

Since my concern is with thought and not with mental processes generally, it would help to have a term that, unlike "mental representation," suggests only representations that play a role in thought or cognition. "Cognitive representation" isn't too bad; however, for stylistic reasons I will generally stick to the traditional "mental representations." Our questions will be "What is it for a mental whatnot to be a representation (i.e., to have a content)?" and "What is it for a mental representation, a whatnot with a content, to have some particular content rather than some other particular content?"

Chapter 2

Mental Representation and Meaning

In this chapter I will take a brief look at the relation between mental representation and meaning generally. Before assessing claims about what it is for a mental state to have a content, it is useful to have some idea of how an account of mental meaning might fit into an account of meaning generally.

Original Meaning

The meaningfulness of some things is often thought to be prior to or more fundamental than the meaningfulness of others. Haugeland (1985, p. 27) writes

> The basic question is: How can thought parcels *mean* anything? The analogy with spoken or written symbols is no help here, since the meanings of these are already derivative from the meanings of thoughts. That is, the meaningfulness of words depends on the prior meaningfulness of our thinking: if the sound (or sequence of letters) "horse" happens to mean a certain kind of animal, that's only because we (English speakers) mean that by it. Now obviously the meaningfulness of thoughts themselves cannot be explained in the same way; for that would be to say that the meanings of our thoughts derive from the meanings of our thoughts, which is circular. Hence some independent account is required.

In this passage, Haugeland expresses the widespread view that meaningfulness generally depends on the meaningfulness of mental states. Mental states, according to this view, have *original meaning*, whereas the meaningfulness of other things (and per-

haps their particular meanings as well) is *derived*, in that they are meaningful, and perhaps have the meanings they have, only because of the meaningfulness and meanings of mental states.

Neo-Gricean Theories

Since the pioneering work of Grice (1957), the idea that meaning generally depends on intentionality has come to form the core of a sophisticated theory of meaning and communication. (See especially Schiffer 1982; Bennett 1975; Lewis 1969; Cummins 1979.) Neo-Gricean accounts of meaning proceed in two phases. In phase one, what a speaker (or, more generally, a user, a "meaner") means by some particular performance is explained in terms of the speaker's intentions. According to neo-Gricean accounts of meaning, the intentions with which we deploy a representation determine what we mean by it, and the beliefs others (and ourselves, especially at later times) have about our communicative intentions constitute their (or our) understanding of it. Phase two of the neo-Gricean account explains conventional (e.g., linguistic) meaning by appealing to a shared plan—a convention in Lewis' (1969) sense—for the communicative use of a representational type: R means M because users of R are parties to a convention whereby those who deploy it mean M by it. In short, representations have meanings only because their users mean various things by them, and meaning something by a representation is a matter of deploying it with the right intentions. Thus, the semantic properties of representations are derived from the intentionality of their users—either directly, or indirectly via the existence of a convention governing their communicative uses.

Could a neo-Gricean theory apply to mental representations as well as to such nonmental representations as linguistic symbols and stop signs? Neo-Griceans hold that meaning ultimately depends on the communicative intentions of communicating agents. A neo-Gricean theory of mental representation, then, would have to hold that someone or something uses mental representations with the intention of communicating something to someone or something. But a person does not use mental

representations with the intention to communicate anything to anyone; indeed, mental representations of the sort standardly featured in the CTC—e.g., a $2\frac{1}{2}$-d sketch or a phonemic representation of a heard utterance—are not used intentionally (or even consciously) at all. Thus, the "communicating agents" required by the theory would have to be subsystems—"sub-personal agents," as Dennett (1978) calls them, or *pro tempore* homunculi (see also Lycan 1981, 1987). These agents would have to have communicative intentions and beliefs in order to mean something by the mental representations they use and in order to enter into conventions governing the communicative uses of those representations.

But this is surely implausible; there is no reason to think that our subpersonal systems (assuming there are such things) *have* beliefs and intentions. Although it is often supposed that subsystems *use* representations in some sense, it is not at all plausible to suppose that they use representations intentionally. Ordinary belief and intention are mysterious enough. We make no explanatory progress by relying on the unexplained and implausible idea that subsystems have communicative intentions and beliefs.[1]

Neo-Gricean theories of meaning can be seen as a species of theory that reduces meaning generally to intentionality. Whereas neo-Gricean theories focus on communicative intentions, there is a tradition, going back to Berkeley and including the later Wittgenstein, that holds that the meaning of a representation is a function of its intended use, where this is construed more broadly than communicative use. The same points just made about neo-Gricean theories apply to the genus generally: They are unpromising as theories of mental representation because they require subpersonal agents with intentions to use mental representations. Thus, "intended-use" theories provide us with no help in explaining mental representation.[2]

Intended-Use Theories without Intentionality

The objection to intended-use theories of mental representation is that they implausibly require subpersonal intentional agents.

This objection could be got around if it were possible to get nonintentional states of some kind to play the role that intentions and beliefs play in intended-use theories. Maybe the nested GOALS and PLANS of AI could be made to do the trick.[3] This may strike some as an attractive idea in any case, since the beliefs and embedded intentions required by Gricean analyses are a bit implausible if construed as ordinary beliefs and intentions; certainly people are seldom if ever conscious of having the required intentions and beliefs.

I can't stop to evaluate this idea here, but it is worth pointing out one source of difficulty. It is no accident that Gricean analyses appeal to beliefs and intentions, for these have the same sort of "wide content" (Putnam 1975) as the linguistic and other representations whose contents these analyses seek to explain. If you think that "water" in your mouth means H_2O and not XYZ (the lookalike stuff on Twin Earth), and if you advocate an intended-use theory of linguistic meaning, then you will want your linguistic meanings to be grounded in mental states that have wide content too. Ordinary beliefs and intentions fit the bill, or so it is often claimed,[4] but it isn't at all clear that the data structures of the CTC can be made to fit the bill (and, as we will see in chapters 8 and 10, they probably cannot).

A more plausible line for intended-use theorists is to reduce nonmental meaning to intentionality, and then to either attempt directly to explain intentionality in some naturalistic way or attempt to reduce intentionality to mental representation and try to deal with *that* naturalistically. It is as part of this last strategy that the RTI especially recommends itself to many: Reduce nonmental meaning to intentionality, and then employ the RTI to reduce intentionality to mental representation. But we need to keep in mind that mental representation as supplied by such theoretical frameworks as the CTC may not be able to bear the burden.

Symmetrical Theories of Meaning

The above quotation from Haugeland envisages an asymmetrical treatment of meaning, i.e., a treatment that accords priority ("originality") to mental meaning. But it is possible to hold that mental and nonmental representation are basically the same. (See, for example, Block 1986 and Millikan 1984.) Theories of this kind must reject the Gricean idea that nonmental representation is grounded in intentionality, for if mental and nonmental representation are the same animal, then mental representation will be grounded in intentionality too, and that, as we saw, is implausible at best. Those who advocate a symmetrical treatment of representation will therefore want to hold either that intentionality and representation are simply independent or that intentionality depends somehow on representation. I am not sure that any one currently adopts the first line. Among those who adopt the second line, two different camps can be discerned: Those who, like Quine (1960) and Davidson (1975), hold that belief and desire are somehow parasitic on language, and those who, like Fodor, seek to ground intentionality in mental representation.

Grounding Intentionality in Mental Representation

There are two basic strategies:

"Localism"   The idea here is to think of each intentional state as grounded in a corresponding mental representation. One can adopt the RTI and then try to attach intentional contents—the contents of beliefs and desires—to mental representations, or one can adopt a modified version of the RTI according to which intentional contents ("wide contents") are the result of subjecting representational contents ("narrow contents") to some further nonpsychological constraint not required for mere representation.

"Globalism"   The idea here is to adopt a conception according to which one's intentional states are grounded in one's total nonintentional psychological state plus, perhaps, some nonpsychological condition. Dennett holds a view like this, as does (I think) Stalnaker (1984).

Conclusion

Philosophy has a lot of roles ready and waiting for mental representation to step into. But whether it can play any of these roles, and if so, which ones, depends on what mental representation *is*. But this question, I contend, can be answered only by examining the scientific theories or frameworks that invoke mental representation as part of their explanatory apparatus. Since there are a number of different frameworks in the running in cognitive science today, we are not likely to get a univocal answer. We won't get *any* answer until we focus on some particular framework and start slogging. The remainder of this book tries to get some of the slogging done by evaluating various philosophical accounts of mental representation to see whether any of them will ground the explanatory role assigned to that concept by orthodox computationalism (i.e., the CTC).

We are now ready to turn to the main questions: What is it for a mental representation to have a content, and what determines what content it has? In the context of the CTC, this is equivalent to asking what makes a data structure a *representation*, and what determines what it represents. And let us just remind ourselves once more that folk psychology and the ordinary language of intentional characterization are NOT the topics.

Chapter 3
Similarity

Several developments in the seventeenth century combined to make the idea that representation is founded on similarity seem difficult to maintain. One of these was the Copernican revolution. Ptolemaics, one supposes, imagined the motions of the planets as they modeled or drew them, and so did their Copernican opponents. But each party imagined matters so differently than the other that, at most, one could possibly have had in mind something similar to the real state of affairs. But then one party or the other (or both) must not have been thinking of the motions of the planets at all! Yet surely the dispute was about the motions of the plants. One party or the other—or perhaps both—*misrepresented* the motions of the planets.

We encounter here for the first time what will be a recurring theme in this book: the difficulty of accounting for *misrepresentation*. The difficulty arises in connection with the similarity view because it seems to make truly radical misrepresentation impossible. Ptolemaic pictures of the planetary motions weren't at all similar to the actual motions, and this seemed to force the conclusion that they were not pictures of the planetary motions but pictures of something else (other Ptolemaic pictures and models?) or of nothing at all. The similarity view seems to allow for misrepresentation only when the dissimilarity is relatively small: If r is to represent x rather than y, then r had better be more similar to x than y; otherwise, similarity can't be the whole story.

A less famous but ultimately more important development

was Galileo's use of geometry to represent nonspatial magnitudes.[1] Consider a body, uniformly accelerated from rest, that
travels a fixed time t. When time runs out, it will have achieved
a velocity v. Now consider a body that travels at a uniform
velocity $v/2$ for the same time t. It turns out that both bodies will
cover the same distance. Galileo's proof of this result involves a
revolutionary use of geometry. In figure 3.1 the height BC of the
triangle/rectangle $EBC/DCBA$ represents the time t. The base EC
of the triangle ECB represents the terminal velocity (v) of the
uniformly accelerated object, and hence the base DC of the
rectangle represents the constant velocity ($v/2$) of the unaccelerated object. The area of the rectangle $DCBA$ represents the
distance traveled by the unaccelerated object (vt), and the area of
the triangle ECB represents the distance traveled by the accelerated body.[2] Proof of the result reduces to the trivial demonstra-
tion that the triangle and the rectangle have the same area.

What is striking about this use of geometry is that lines represent not trajectories or distances but times and velocities. *Areas*,
not lines, represent distances. Nowhere is the path of the object
through space represented. Similarity evidently gives us no
handle on what makes Galileo's diagram a representation of

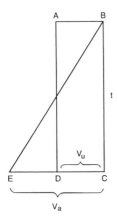

Figure 3.1
Galileo's diagram.

mechanical magnitudes and their relations. What we need is something radically different. The crucial factor seems to be that, given Galileo's interpretation, the laws of geometry discipline the representations and their relations to each other in the same way that the laws of nature discipline the mechanical magnitudes and their interactions.[3] We will return to this important theme in chapter 8.

Descartes put the finishing touches on this story by discovering a way to do geometry with symbols instead of pictures. Descartes' analytic geometry allows us to represent spatial things with equations. Nothing is more obvious than that the Cartesian equation for a sphere doesn't *resemble* a sphere.

As striking as all these examples are, it is possible (just) to dismiss them as cases of nonmental representation on a par with language. After all, it was obvious all along that all representation couldn't be grounded in similarity, since language is an obvious counterexample. There were, of course, half-hearted efforts to see linguistic representation in terms of similarity. But words seldom sound (or look) like what they mean. Still, language and other nonmental cases could be, and generally were, defused by adopting some form of the intended-use theory, leaving original meanings attached to things in the head—images or inFORMed mind stuff—things comfortably dependent on similarity for their status as representations.

For Locke, however, there was at least one scientific development that didn't admit of this otherwise admirable solution: atomism's introduction of the concept of a secondary quality. By Locke's lights, anyway, secondary qualities seem to be explicit cases of mental representation without resemblance (*Essay Concerning Human Understanding*, II, viii). This led Locke to develop an account of mental representation that did not depend on similarity, but on covariance. This idea—an idea that enjoys considerable popularity today—will be the subject of the next chapter.

Similarity Critiqued

Computationalists must dismiss similarity theories of representation out of hand; nothing is more obvious than that data

Figure 3.2
Descartes representing a sphere.

structures don't resemble what they represent. Still, it is worth taking a few pages to rehearse some more general problems with the idea that mental representation is grounded in similarity.

The Problem of the Brain as Medium
The most obvious difficulty with the similarity theory is that it seems incompatible with physicalism. If mental representations are physical things, and if representation is grounded in similarity, then there must be physical things in the brain that are similar to (i.e., that share properties with) the things they represent. This problem could be kept at bay only so long as mind-stuff was conceived of as nonphysical. The idea that we could get redness and sphericity in the mind loses its plausibility if this means we have to get it in the brain. When I look at a red ball, a red sphere doesn't appear in my brain. If the ball is a rubber ball, it seems the brain will have to be made of rubber, or at least be elastic. And what about furry tabby cats?

But perhaps we can find a way to get along with less than the real thing. Perhaps something with a kind of *restricted* similarity would do. After all, pictures can represent three-dimensional things without themselves *being* three-dimensional. And isn't pictorial representation—the sort of thing we call "representational art"—grounded in similarity? Of course the nature of the representational medium restricts the kind and degree of similarity that is possible. But that doesn't prevent some representations in that medium from being more similar to some things in the world than others. A cartoon drawing of Sylvester the cat is more similar to Granny than to Tweety Bird, and more similar to Sylvester than to either of those, even though it isn't furry and doesn't chase birds. Cartoon drawings are limited with respect to the kinds of similarity to the world they can exhibit, but they do remarkably well for all that. In principle, anyway, the same point applies to brain processes.

The trouble with this idea is that "restricted" similarity isn't really similarity (actual sharing of properties); it is only "perceived" similarity. When thinking of similarity, it is often useful to ask yourself whether the things said to be similar could literally have the same properties. Cartoon cats cannot resemble cats in point of furriness, because cartoon cats cannot be furry. Cartoon cats can only *look* furry—*to us.* Cartoon cats manage to represent cats because they *look like cats to us.* Cats and cartoon cats are, up to a point and in certain respects, perceptually equivalent. A cartoon cat in the Sunday comics isn't really similar to a cat in any nonpsychological sense of similarity.[4] The same point applies to brain states: They aren't similar to cats. At best, highly stylized pictures of them might look similar to cats *to us,* in the same way an ink blot or a cloud might look like a cat to us. But this is evidently of no use to the similarity theorist, since perceived similarity is evidently an intentional relation and hence presupposes mental meaning rather than explaining it. Moreover, perceived similarity is useless unless there is something or someone in a position to perceive both the representation and the representandum. But in spite of loose talk of "perceiving" images, it is clear that one does not perceive one's mental representations in the sense in which one perceives cats and red rubber balls.

Of course, a difference in "medium" doesn't rule out all genuine similarity. A clay statue can literally have the same shape and size as a bronze statue. It can even have the same mass. But it cannot have the same mass and the same density, and it cannot have the same melting temperature, and so on. And of course it cannot be made of the same stuff. Once we weed out merely observer-relative "perceived" similarities, it is clear that there isn't a hope of enough genuine similarity's remaining between brain states and the enormous variety of things we represent to underwrite mental representation. When we get down to cases, the idea often doesn't even seem to make sense. After all, what in the brain could literally have the same phonetic properties as a linguistic utterance?[5]

The Problem of Abstraction
Even if we ignore the fact that a difference in medium between representation and representandum is bound to rule out all but the most shallow similarities, the doctrine that representation is ultimately grounded in similarity suffers from a serious conceptual defect: Similarity theories cannot deal with abstraction.

To see how this problem arises in a concrete case, suppose that our mental representations are images, and suppose that there is no problem about how images could resemble things in the world. There is still a problem about how images could function as abstract ideas: How could an image of a dog mean any dog whatever, rather than some particular dog (namely the one to which it is most similar)?

As Jonathan Bennett (1971) points out, the problem isn't *completely hopeless*; images can simply be, as it were, silent about certain matters. For example, it is possible to imagine your car without thereby imagining the license plate down to the number and the name of the state. Your image, then, will equally "agree to" any car that differs from yours only in license plate.

The amount of abstraction available from images, however, is limited. We cannot, as Berkeley pointed out in the introduction to the *Principles of Human Knowledge,* imagine a triangle without thereby failing to produce an image that will agree equally to any triangle. Ditto for cats and neckties: Either you imagine stripes or you don't, and either way you're going to miss some of the best cats and ties. So images won't do as abstract ideas—as representations that have, in principle, open-ended extensions.[6]

It doesn't take too much to see that the problem isn't limited to images; anything that is supposed to represent by resemblance is going to suffer the same fate. Indeed, anything *physical* is going to do worse than mental images, because physical things can't simply be "missing" a property; every determinable is going to have some determinate value.[7] Finding a physical object that is equally similar to all cats but more similar to any cat than to any noncat is *conceptually* out of the question. Similarity can't hope to underwrite abstraction, and representation without abstraction is, as Locke pointed out in book III of the *Essay,* not worth bothering about.

The problem of abstract representation is this: How can a representation "agree to" (represent) a whole class of things that differ widely from one another on many dimensions? How, for example, can we represent all and only vegetables? Similarity is no help here, because the brain isn't a vegetable and because nothing is *only* a vegetable. Anything you happen to pick as a vegetable representation (especially a nonvegetable such as a brain state) will be similar to nonvegetables in a huge number of irrelevant respects. Thus, another way to see the problem of abstraction is this: How do we rule out resemblance in irrelevant respects?

To see how this problem might be solved, consider how simulacra might enter into an account of color recognition. How might we design a system to do the job? As a crude first pass, we might give the system a set of plastic chips of various colors, with color words printed on them. To identify the color of something, the system would find the best match in its supply of chips and display the word. Now, of course this works fine if the system knows to match the *color* of the target to the *color* of the chip. But suppose it is simply a "similarity detector." What is to prevent it from, say, matching its round chips to round targets and its square chips to square targets? After all, it has to *have* such chips if it is going to be able to deal with shape as well as color. A simple solution is to make sure that the only similarities the system can detect are similarities in color. But then what makes the blue chip represent *blue* in this system isn't just the fact that it is blue (and hence similar to blue things); it also depends on the fact that it is used by a device that ignores everything but color. The very same chip, used by a device that ignores everything but shape, represents (say) *round*. Moreover, it is clear on reflection that, even in the color case, the color of the chip is inessential. What is essential is only that something in the system with the word "blue" printed on it should get sent to the display module *when and only when* the system is given a blue target.[8] This is the idea that Locke exploited to develop the core of a theory of representation based on covariance (note the italicized phrase in the previous sentence) rather than on similarity. It is thus no accident that Locke was led to covariance; if you are interested, as Locke was, in the problem of abstraction, there is a natural and compelling route from similarity to covariance. For Locke, the problem of abstraction and the problem posed by secondary qualities lead to the same place.

Chapter 4
Covariance I: Locke

Plot

The idea that mental representation is grounded in covariance has recently been worked out by a number of philosophers, most notably Fodor (1987) and Dretske (1981). However, the central thesis—that causal links between mental representations and the world determine the semantic content of mental representations—is widespread. I cannot hope to deal separately with all the important variations on this idea. Instead, I will begin by constructing and criticizing a kind of prototype that I find in book III of Locke's *Essay Concerning Human Understanding*. I think Locke did, in fact, hold something like the theory I will expound, but I don't really care. What I want is a clear and fairly simple version of the sort of theory that founds representation on covariance. The theory I attribute to Locke satisfies this requirement admirably. I am convinced that contemporary versions of covariance theories, including those of Fodor and Dretske, are easily understood and critiqued once we understand the basic flaws in the simple theory I attribute to Locke. The idea, then, is that this chapter will function as a kind of warmup. Getting the basic ideas and moves down pat in this somewhat artificial setting will facilitate discussion of the more sophisticated versions of Fodor and Dretske in the next two chapters.

Locke on the Semantics of Mental Representation

Locke, unlike Berkeley and Hume, saw clearly that representation could not be founded on resemblance. What, then, *does* it rest on? Locke's answer is that it rests on covariance: Our simple ideas are adequate because they are regular and natural productions in us of external causes. The idea we have when we look at a white thing is an idea of whiteness—a representation of whiteness—because it is the idea white things naturally cause us to have.

Evidently, however, not every case of covariation is a case of representation. Sunburns don't represent exposure to ultraviolet rays. To deal with this problem, Locke had recourse to the following idea: Covariation is representation when the representor (the idea or symbol or whatever) has the right sort of cognitive function. The thing is a representation in virtue of having the right function, and the covariance establishes the specific content.[1]

To see how this works, we need a systematic context—a sketch of a cognitive system—to anchor talk of cognitive functions. (See Cummins 1975a.) To this end, consider Locke's theory of the classificatory use of general words. In book III of the *Essay*, Locke expounds a theory that explains the semantic properties of communicative symbols in terms of the semantic properties of mental representations. For example, on Locke's theory it is the fact that a general word is conventionally associated with a certain abstract idea that gives that term its satisfaction conditions.

Locke was impressed with the tension between two facts: (i) any symbol can have any meaning whatever—words don't fit the world as keys fit locks. (ii) Nevertheless, words can be used incorrectly and falsely. How can (ii) be true, given (i)? How can "cat" be the right word for Graycat, given that the word "cat" doesn't *fit* Graycat any better than any other word? Locke's answer was that when we learn English we learn that, in our language community, the term "cat" is conventionally associated with an abstract idea (concept) that bears a natural, nonconventional semantic relation of *agreement* to all and only the cats. Abstract ideas *do* fit the world as keys fit locks, and words "stand for" abstract ideas in virtue of a purely conventional association.

Locke has given us, or can be construed as having provided, a

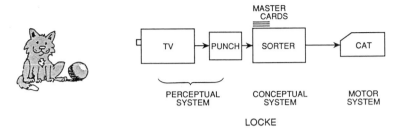

Figure 4.1
The LOCKE machine recognizing a cat.

computational account of the classificatory use of general terms. This becomes obvious if we imagine a concrete instantiation. Consider, then, the mechanical device LOCKE (figure 4.1). LOCKE is equipped with a TV camera hooked up to some input modules (in the sense of Fodor 1983), which in turn are hooked up to a card punch. When the TV camera is pointed at something, a punch card called a concrete idea of sense or a *percept* is produced. Percepts are fed into a sorter, which compares them with a stack of master cards called abstract ideas or *concepts*. When a percept matches a concept—i.e., when the percept contains at least all the holds the concept contains—LOCKE displays the term written on the back of the concept. Any word can be written on the back of any concept; that is a matter of convention. But once the words are printed on the concepts, everything else is a matter of physics. Concepts, of course, can have control functions other than the one just described, and percepts needn't be visual. Moreover, concepts are made from percepts, according to Locke. But enough; what we have will do for the purpose at hand.[2]

Given this sketch of a part of the human cognitive system, we can put the notion of covariance to work to define representation. What makes a given concept the cat-concept is the fact that it is the thing that matches percepts of cats. What makes something a percept of a cat is just that it has some features (some pattern of punches) that percepts come to have in the system when, only when, and because the system is in perceptual contact with a cat. Cats cause Locke's perceptual system to generate percepts with a characteristic punch pattern. When it finds (or constructs) a master card that matches that pattern, it writes 'cat' on the back, because that is the pattern that identifies the presence of cats to the system and hence the pattern wanted as the meaning of 'cat'. (It does this, we may suppose, by a kind of trial and error, trying various words on various cards until it is able to substantially avoid error messages from its peers.) If there is a pattern of punches that shows up on percept cards when, only when, and because the TV camera is pointed at a cat, then that pattern, wherever it occurs in the system, represents cats. Being a cat representation is being something that is, in perceptual contexts, a litmus test for cat presence. For future reference, the idea is briefly expressed as follows:

(L1) x represents y in LOCKE $=_{df}$ x is a punch pattern that occurs in a percept when, only when, and because LOCKE is confronted by y (whiteness, a cat, whatever).

There is, of course, a problem about how to spell out "confronted by" in a non-question-begging way, for the only thing that looks a sure bet is to say that LOCKE is confronted by a cat, or whiteness, just in case a corresponding percept is produced. But a corresponding percept is just one that has the right representational content. I suppose the best strategy is to pass the buck to the psychophysicists, trusting them to identify in some nonintentional way some causal conditions sufficient for percept production. In practice this is likely to be circular, since the only way psychophysicists are going to discover such conditions is by correlating them with the "corresponding" percepts. But in principle (philosopher's friend!) it doesn't have to go that way, as the example of LOCKE shows; we can simply correlate a punch pattern *qua* punch pattern with a set of conditions sufficient to produce it (given proper functioning of LOCKE).

Notice how the theory works: If something with the right role in the system—the right function—covaries with something else, then we have not only representation but also a specific content. Locke's theory begins with the plausible (perhaps inevitable) idea that the things that mediate cat recognition in the system must be the cat representations. To put this idea to work, we have had to sketch enough of a functional analysis of the recognition system to identify the relevant things: punch patterns on percept cards. This is surely the right way to solve the Problem of Representations. But the theory goes farther; it proceeds to read off a solution to the Problem of *Representation—viz.*, L1.[3]

The essential points about the theory, from Locke's point of view, are (i) that it does away with resemblance as the ground of representation and (ii) that it solves the problem of abstraction. Let us take a moment to understand how this is accomplished.

Resemblance avoided   In discussing a simple color-recognition system in the last chapter, we encountered the following problem: How is the system to avoid matching the round blue chip to round targets instead of blue ones? The obvious solution is to design the system so that it is insensitive to everything but color. But then it is easy to see how to make resemblance drop out of the picture, for what matters is only that the system produce something with 'blue' printed on it in response to blue things. Whether that something is itself blue is quite irrelevant; the causal origin and the functional role of the thing—the fact that it gets produced by blue things and the fact that it drives the "speech" system (and other motor and cognitive systems) appropriate—are what count.

Abstraction achieved   Once we cease to think of the relation between representation and representandum in terms of similarity and begin to think in terms of covariance, the problem of abstraction has a simple solution. A master card (concept) that has a pattern of punches that occurs in a percept when and only when the system is confronted by blue has something that will match (have the same punch pattern as) every adequate percept of a blue thing, and in that sense will "agree with" (Locke's term) each and every blue thing. No such solution is available to the resemblance theorist, because nothing can resemble all and only the blue things. But something can be the "regular and natural effect" of blue on the system, and hence occur in the system's percepts when and only when blue is present to it.

Misrepresentation

The fundamental difficulty facing Lockean theories is to explain how misrepresentation is possible. To see why this is a difficulty, try to describe a case of misrepresentation. Suppose LOCKE is confronted by Graycat but generates a dog-percept (i.e., a percept with the feature *D*). Then it is not true that *D* occurs in a percept when, only when, and because a dog is present, since no dog is present and the current percept has feature *D*. Hence, *D* doesn't represent doghood, and LOCKE has not generated a dog-percept, contrary to hypothesis. LOCKE cannot misrecognize Graycat as a dog—not because LOCKE is so clever, but because mirepresentation is an incoherent notion given L1, the target theory of representation. Since it is possible (indeed inevitable) to sometimes misrecognize cats as dogs, something must be wrong.

Lockeans, I think, have just one way of dealing with this problem: idealization.[4] This can take one of two forms: idealizing away from malfunctions and idealizing away from suboptimal conditions of perceptual recognition.

Malfunctions and Misrepresentations
It is tempting to regard misrepresentation as something that arises from malfunction: Perhaps if LOCKE were functioning properly, it wouldn't misrecognize Graycat as a dog. We can exploit this idea by defining representation as follows:

> (L2) *x* represents *y* in LOCKE $=_{df}$ were LOCKE functioning properly, punch pattern *x* would occur in a percept when, only when, and because LOCKE is confronted by *y*.

L2 allows for misrepresentation because it makes having a representational content a modal property of punch patterns—a property a punch patter can have even if LOCKE never succeeds in recognizing something corresponding to that content. Perhaps it always malfunctions when confronted by cats. Nevertheless, it could still be true that *were LOCKE to function properly*, pattern *C would* occur in a percept when, only when, and because the system is confronted by a cat. Given this revision, it isn't actual covariance that matters; it is the covariance that would obtain were LOCKE functioning properly.   Perhaps, like many AI systems, LOCKE seldom functions properly.

Given our focus on the CTC, the trouble with this response to the problem of misrepresentation is that, according to the CTC, the most obvious and everyday cases of perceptual misrepresentation—*viz.*, the illusions—are not cases of malfunction but cases of proper functioning in abnormal circumstances. What happens is that the normal functioning of the system in an abnormal situation results in a misrepresentation. For example, subjects looking into the Ames Room (figure 4.2) misrepresent the relative heights of things in the opposite corners.   But the problem isn't that the visual system suddenly breaks down in some way when one looks into the Ames Room; the problem is

Figure 4.2
The Ames Room. The dog is really much smaller than the child!

rather that the visual system computes the relative heights of the things in the room from, among other things, the assumption that the room has square corners.[5] The same principle holds even more obviously in purely cognitive cases; for example, the detective who draws the most rational conclusion given the available evidence may yet arrest the wrong person. In such a case, normal functioning—even optimal functioning—guarantees misrepresentation if the evidence is inadequate in some way.

If cognition rests on computation, as the CTC assumes, then there is an important respect in which error is essential to a well-designed cognitive system: The computational problems faced by a system with finite resources—especially memory and time—can succeed only by taking short-cuts. Such a system must employ algorithms that rest on fallible assumptions—for example, that objects in space are rigid (Ullman 1979), that corners of a room are "square," that the future will resemble the past in the respects chosen by conceptually salient features, that other agents are rational and in fact know what they are in position to know, or that objects don't come in transparent pairs (hold up your finger in your field of vision and focus on something beyond it), etc.

Traditional epistemology typically attempts to idealize away from resource constraints. Research in AI strongly suggests that this is a false idealization: When you try to add in resource constraints afterward, you always wind up redesigning the system from scratch. Epistemology for God and epistemology for us are two different things. God never had to worry about recognizing tigers *in time to evade them*.

Ideal Circumstances for Perception
Assimilating misrepresentation to malfunction, then, yields a concept of misrepresentation that undermines computationalist explanations of misrepresentation. Still, reflection on the critique just rehearsed suggests another cure. The core of that critique is that misrepresentation often occurs as the result of proper (even ideal) functioning in *less-than-ideal circumstances*. Misrepresentation seems (in these cases, anyway) to be due to a departure from

ideal circumstances. This suggests that we revise the definition as follows:

(L3) x represents y in LOCKE = $_{df}$ were LOCKE functioning properly and circumstances ideal, x would occur in a percept when, only when, and because LOCKE is confronted by y.

L3 evidently allows for truly radical misrepresentation of the sort imagined in Cartesian Demon scenarios: If all my perceptual states are caused directly by the Demon, then conditions are never ideal. But it is still possible to represent cats, say, because it might still be the case that, *were* conditions ideal, the relevant pattern would occur when, only when, and because a cat is present. I emphasize this point in order to make it clear that L3 (and L2, for that matter) accommodates misrepresentation by going modal and thereby putting meanings in the head.[6]

Not only is this a natural way for the account to bend under pressure from misperception cases; it is really the *only* way it can bend. The *essence* of the position is that something is a representation of a cat in virtue of having some feature that is, in percepts, an effect of cat presence and not of anything else. It has to be something that occurs in percepts because a *cat* is present. If it occurs because something else is present—a clever cat robot, or a dog, a raccoon, or a koala bear—then the account is going to attach the wrong content to the punch pattern in question, with the result that nothing will count as a cat representation. But no occurrence in a perceptual system has a chance of being the effect of cats (or anything else interesting) *exclusively* unless conditions are ideal.[7] Under *real* conditions, error is the price you *must* pay for computational tractability.

The obvious first question that L3 invites is whether it is really possible to assimilate *all* misrepresentation to failures of one sort of idealization or the other, i.e., to improper function or to less-than-ideal "circumstances." My own view is that it is not possible. I will pursue this point shortly. For the moment, I want to pursue a different sort of objection: When combined with a fundamental empirical assumption of the CTC, L3 leads us in a circle and is therefore incompatible with the CTC.

The assumption in question is that cognitive systems manage to get into states that reliably covary with distal features of the environment because of their representational resources: What the system does is *infer* the distal situation from current data (proximal stimuli, if the problem is perceptual) and *a great deal of knowledge stored as data structures.*

To see why this sorts ill with L3, we need to scrutinize this business of ideal circumstances. According to the CTC, what is likely to be involved? Under *what* conditions is the system likely to produce percepts with features that reliably covary with some *distal* feature? The CTC has it (indeed, this was the fundamental claim of the so-called cognitive revolution) that cognitive systems are able to get into states that reliably covary with distal features because of their stored knowledge.[8] For LOCKE, what this means is that, in addition to good lighting and that sort of thing, the perceptual system is going to have to have access to a rich fund of *knowledge about what sorts of distal features are likely to produce which sorts of signals at the output end of the TV camera. The idea (*THE* idea) is that the system is able to reason from the TV-output (transduced proximal stimuli) and its fund of *knowledge to a conclusion about the responsible distal feature.[9] The system, in fact, executes a program that has access to a representation of the transduced proximal stimuli and to all this *knowledge, and that program computes a representation of the distal feature. That representation, in turn, drives the card-punch, which produces a percept. This, at any rate, is the story the CTC directs us to tell. Thus (to echo Fodor), if we are after the notion of representation that underwrites computational explanations in psychology, we had better take this story seriously.

For present purposes, we can sum up the implications of the story as follows: *If the percept is to be adequate, the mediating *knowledge had better be adequate too.* Of course, the transduced proximal stimulus has got to be high-grade as well. That will require a properly functioning TV camera, and good light, and appropriate distances and angles, and so on. But all that won't be nearly enough. A big part of what must be the case if the occurrence of *x* in a percept is to covary with the occurrence of *y* in the environment is that the mediating *knowledge must be there and must be adequate. No matter how good the stimulus

and how well the mechanism functions, suboptimal mediating
*knowledge—a pack of lies, for instance—is going to make it
impossible for LOCKE to produce percepts with features that
reliably occur when, only when, and because there is whiteness,
or a cat, present. But it follows from this that the relevant notion
of "ideal circumstances" to which F3 appeals is, in large part, a
matter of the system's having the right *knowledge—i.e., the
right representations; representations with the right content.
And *that* means we cannot fill out L3 without making liberal use
of the very notion that L3 is supposed to explain.

It is worth belaboring this point a bit. A computational system
of the sort favored by the CTC has no serious hope of arriving at
the truth about even very common *perceptual* matters without the
help of a formidable background of *knowledge. It is fundamental to the computational approach to perception that perceptual
systems must make use of a very considerable and sophisticated
base of *knowledge about the world, including its own
"specifications," in order to construct reliable percepts. Language perception is the most celebrated case, but any perceptual
system that solves the problem of perceptual constancy is essentially the same; a central claim of the CTC is that the only hope of
mapping proximal stimuli onto distal stimuli is to use *knowledge of how proximal stimuli are generated to arrive at a "best
hypothesis" concerning the distal situation. To define representation in terms of the optimal functioning of such a system is to
presuppose the very notion one is trying to define, for such
systems are *specified*, in large and essential part, by the tacit
*knowledge they embody (i.e., by their representational re-
sources). According to the CTC, perceptual and other cognitive
systems are able to generate reliable indicators of distal features
because of their cognitive resources—that is, because they are
representational systems. If you define representation in terms of
the ideal behavior of a certain kind of system, you must be
prepared to specify the kind of system you have in mind. But the
CTC holds that there is no way to specify a system that has a hope
of reliably indicating the sort of facts we are capable of representing without making liberal use of the notion of representation.

That, to repeat, is what the cognitive revolution and the defeat of behaviorism was originally all about. A program isn't enough; to understand such things as speech perception you need to specify the relevant *knowledge (data) structures. Indeed, it is hardly exaggerating to say that, from a CTC perspective, the problem of (say) speech perception just *is* the problem of discovering what *knowledge is required, and in what form it must exist to mediate the required inferences.[10]

It might seem that the Lockean doesn't owe us an account of ideal circumstances.[11] The Lockean says, in effect: "Being a representation—having a content—is essentially a matter of having the right sort of function. Which content a representation has is determined by what its tokening in the system would covary with under ideal conditions. Thus, what you do to ascribe content is point to the right sort of thingamabob—a punch pattern in a percept card, say—and ask what would covary with the occurrence of that thingamabob if circumstances were ideal. Why isn't that clear enough?"

It is clear enough as far as it goes, but it doesn't go very far. We might concede a kind of formal correctness to the definition, but it has no explanatory value except insofar as we have some conception of what is meant by ideal circumstances. To see this— to see that the explanatory value of L3 depends on what conception of ideal circumstances one has—just consider the default conception one *does* have, viz., that conditions are ideal when they are such as to guarantee (or maximize the chances of) success. On this conception, circumstances are ideal for perceiving (say) cats only if the system, when confronted by a cat, produces (or is maximally likely to produce) a representation with the content CAT. This understanding of ideal circumstances plainly renders L3 circular. So, evidently, if L3 is to tell us anything useful, we must bring some other conception of ideal circumstances to bear. Moreover, it must be a conception that does not depend on a prior understanding of the notion being defined, or of *any* other semantic/intentional concept, since Lockeans typically propose to use mental representation to explain all that other stuff.

What can this conception be? It cannot be the default conception, as we have just seen. And, as we saw earlier, it can't be the one that falls out of the CTC either, for that conception relies heavily (as does everything that falls out of that theory) on the very notion of representation we are trying to explicate. My own view is that these exhaust the plausible alternatives; hence my claim that L3 leads us in a circle when combined with the CTC. The Lockean wants to explain representational content in S by reference to the covariance that would emerge if things were NICE FOR S. This helps only if we understand what it is for things to be NICE FOR S. The difficulty is that the CTC gives us formulations of what it is to be NICE FOR S that make use of the very notion of representational content that the Lockean is trying to define.

Of course, Lockeans won't give up that easily. They have, I think, two more cards to play. One is a kind of semantic reductionism, and the other depends on the notion of inexplicit mental content (i.e., mental content that is not the content of some representation). These don't represent *plausible* alternatives, but that remains to be argued. Let us take them in turn.

Semantic Reductionism
The situation is this: The Lockean needs to tell us under what conditions LOCKE will be able to punch a certain pattern—the *c*-pattern, let's call it—into a percept when and only when confronted by a cat. Under normal conditions, LOCKE will not be able to do this. It is no mean feat, after all. LOCKE needs all the help it can get. Computationalist theories all agree about what sort of help LOCKE needs: lots of the right *knowledge. But if Lockeans go that route, they render their account circular.

To avoid being circular, Lockeans must specify ideal conditions in a way that does not presuppose content assignments to states of the cognitive system. They cannot, therefore, appeal to all that *knowledge. Thus, it is natural for a Lockean to ask what can be achieved *without it*. What sort of perceptual successes can one expect the system to achieve *in complete *ignorance*, as it were?

The inevitable move is some version of reductionism. We "begin" with simple perceptual features. A simple perceptual feature is, by definition, the representation of something the properly functioning system cannot be mistaken about (given the right lighting and so on) precisely because it is a representation whose construction is immune to influences from whatever *knowledge a system might have. Simple perceptual features are, in fact, direct correlates of transduced proximal stimuli; they represent properties that can be transduced.[12] For these cases, L3 works as it stands. We then move on to "complex features." Constructing these *does*, of course, require the mediation of *knowledge, but that is OK because we have explicitly provided for some (or something out of which it can be built) by providing for simple perceptual features. And so on.

This reply avoids the objection, but at a considerable two-part price:

(i) There have to *be* simple perceptual features, i.e., perceptual features that represent properties that can be transduced.

(ii) Percepts the construction of which requires mediation by *knowledge must require only such *knowledge as can ultimately be expressed solely in terms of representations of simple features. The punch pattern for CAT must be a superposition of punch patterns that represent simple perceptual properties.

It is worth emphasizing that (ii) must be interpreted in a strongly reductionist way. Under ideal conditions, the system must be infallible. Confronting whiteness must be nomically sufficient and necessary for the occurrence of the w-feature in percepts. Hence, the transduced proximal stimulus, plus *knowledge, plus nonpsychological laws of nature must *entail* (not just make highly probable; not just reliably indicate) that there is whiteness out there. Remember the "when and only when" in L3. "When": If a cat occurs and the c-pattern doesn't occur, then the possibility exists that only orange cats, or only Graycat, excite the c-pattern. "Only when": If the c-pattern occurs sometimes when it is a dog out there, then there is no principled reason not to say that the c-pattern represents CAT-or-DOG. Thus, the concept CAT must *reduce to* concepts that apply to simple perceptual properties— i.e., to proximal stimuli.

Good luck. The literature since Descartes is littered with bankrupt programs that found this price too high.[13] If you want to get all your content out of representations of simple perceptual properties, you are welcome to try; however, you would do well to keep in mind that this strategy has a dismal track record. That is good enough for me; I don't propose to rake it all up again.

Inexplicit Content: An Alternative Reply
As we saw in chapter 1, natural and artificial information-processing systems can be semantically characterized—characterized, in fact, in terms of propositional contents—even though the propositional content in question is not explicitly represented in the system. I call the object of such characterization *inexplicit content* to distinguish it from content that is explicitly represented in the system.

Inexplicit content is "in" the system without being represented in it. It is thus open to a Lockean to claim (with little plausibility, as we will see) that a cognitive system doesn't require *knowledge to mediate perception. It does require content of a sort, of course, but nothing *explicitly represented* is required. The relevant facts about the system are facts to be specified in terms of inexplicit content. Since inexplicit content is not represented content, a definition of representation that presupposes inexplicit content is not circular or regressive. This reply blocks the critique just leveled against L3, for it demonstrates that in specifying ideal conditions for perception we *can* presuppose contentful background states of LOCKE so long as the presupposed content is *inexplicit*.

Empirically, this is not a very plausible idea, as I said a moment ago. Such things as the rigidity and continuity assumptions exploited in vision (Marr 1972; Ullman 1979) may well be implicit in the architecture of the visual system in some way (Pylyshyn 1984, p. 215).[14] Much of the information that a perceptual system brings to bear on a particular perceptual problem is unlearned and fixed. But much is not. Language perception is a good case in point. The ability to perceive the phonemes, words, phrases, structures, etc. of one's language is, to a large extent, acquired.

Foreign speech sounds like rapid, continuous, unorganized noise, but this changes drastically as you learn the language. Now, the CTC accounts for learning—as opposed to other kinds of psychological change (maturation, trauma, disease)—as the result of the acquisition of new *knowledge. Changes in architecture (program) don't count as learning, for they are not computationally driven. Thus, if acquiring a new language is learning (as it seems to be), it is not, according to the CTC, a matter of acquiring a new architecture, and hence it is not something to be explained in terms of changes in inexplicit content. The perceptual skills involved in understanding speech are therefore mediated to a significant extent by *knowledge. Much the same goes, I suspect, for other domains. The cases of perception mediated only by inexplicit content probably do not go very far beyond the cases of simple transduction.

But it doesn't really matter; even if we concede that perception is mediated only by inexplicit content and not by explicit representations, we will have saved the letter but not the spirit of Lockean covariation theories. Lockean theories are supposed to explicate what it is for a cognitive system—its states, processes, or whatever—to have semantic properties. The assumption is that cognitive representations are the fundamental bearers of such properties. If Lockean approaches are construed so as to presuppose inexplicit content, they fail to address the fundamental problem they are designed to solve: the problem of what it is or something mental to have a semantic property.

Covariation and Inexplicit Content
But perhaps we can work out a Lockean approach to the problem of inexplicit content. If so, and if we can get around the fact that perception mediating *knowledge is often learned and hence not inexplicit, it could still be maintained that mental content is ultimately grounded in covariance.

Inexplicit content is part of what Pylyshyn (1984) calls the biologically fixed functional architecture.[15] It isn't something that comes and goes in the system, at least not as the result of cognitive factors. It is, therefore, essential to a particular cognitive system; change the inexplicit content descriptions and you have described a different cognitive system (though perhaps one that is realized in the same biological system). Given this, if we are going to make use of the idea of covariation we are going to have to trade on the idea that a certain kind of functional architecture occurs when and only when the world exhibits a certain feature, or when and only when a certain condition obtains.

This is plainly going to fail for artificial computational systems, for we are constantly building systems whose architectures embody horribly false assumptions. Every logical bug is a case in point. What is more serious, every program that falls victim to the frame problem or fails to capture the flexibility of human reasoning is a case in point. Every time we build a system that fails in some way because it is programmed wrong (rather than merely misinformed), we instantiate an architecture that embodies false assumptions. It is, to say the least, difficult to avoid this. That, in part, is what makes AI a challenging empirical discipline.

I think we should be impressed by the obvious hopelessness of a covariance account of inexplicit content in artificial systems, for it seems clear that anyone who accepts the CTC must suppose that appeals to representation have just the same explanatory role in artificial systems as in natural ones. That, in fact, is one way of stating a fundamental assumption of computationalism. Thus, if an account of representation doesn't work for artificial systems—if, in fact, it is patently silly for such systems—then it isn't an account of the concept of representation that underlies the CTC.

This, by my lights, is enough to kill Lockean accounts of inexplicit content in the context of the CTC stone dead. Nevertheless, I am going to ignore the problem raised by artificial systems and push forward with the discussion of natural systems, because I think something interesting emerges.

If we are going to make use of the idea of covariation, then (as I said above) we are going to have to trade on the idea that a certain kind of functional architecture occurs when and only when the world exhibits a certain feature, or when and only when a certain condition obtains. What this gives us is something like the following (assuming, for now, propositional contents):

(L4)   *S* has (embodies?) an inexplicit content with truth condition $C =_{df}$ the sort of functional architecture *S* exhibits occurs (persists?) iff *C* obtains.

Thus, for example, an architecture inexplicitly embodies the rigidity assumption just in case architectures like it occur (persist?) if and only if the rigidity assumption is in fact satisfied.

One would have to be a wildly enthusiastic adaptationist to believe this, even about biological systems. Surely satisfaction of the rigidity assumption isn't sufficient for the occurrence of the relevant architecture. I suppose the assumption is satisfied on Mars, but I'm quite sure the architectures in question don't occur there. Nor is satisfaction of the assumption necessary for the occurrence of the architecture; lots of interesting biological features occur that aren't adaptations. If this happens in the cognitive realm—and I don't see any reason to suppose that it couldn't— then the architecture could occur in environments that don't satisfy the assumption.

To get around this, the Lockean will have to resort to the old idealization trick: Perhaps under ideal evolutionary conditions, ... [16] Still, this may look promising; after all, *adaptation* isn't an intentional notion, and the mechanisms responsible for the occurrence of a certain kind of architecture do not depend on the mediation of *knowledge, and that looks like progress. I suppose it is progress, but it is progress down the wrong road.

The problem is that the sort of covariance envisioned by L4 just isn't what is behind inexplicit content. What makes it appropriate to describe the architecture of the visual system in terms of (e.g.) the rigidity assumption is, minimally, that *the system wouldn't work if the assumption didn't hold*. If things seen didn't generally remain more or less rigid under spatial transformation, the system would constantly misrepresent things. *That* is why it makes sense to say that the assumption is, as it were, built into the architecture. It is wired up to operate as if it were reasoning from *knowledge that included the rigidity assumption. The vision program exploits the constraint in that its proper operation presupposes that the constraint is satisfied.

The evolutionary story is plausible only because we know that a system with the architecture in question will work well only if the rigidity assumption is approximately satisfied, for the evolutionary story depends on the idea that such architectures will not survive—will not be replicated over many generations—unless the conditions for their working well are met. This is a pretty dubious idea, even under the assumption of ideal evolutionary conditions (whatever that may come to); but that is not my point. My point is that the evolutionary story assumes that a system with the architecture in question will work well only if the rigidity assumption is satisfied. But if we have assumed that, we have assumed all we need to assume for the relevant inexplicit content; the evolutionary story *presupposes* the inexplicit content attribution! Covariation, and the evolutionary scenario that allows us to trot it out, simply drop out as irrelevant. I don't know if we should count this as a circularity in L4, but I do think it renders L4 intellectually uninformative. It just can't help you understand what it is to have an inexplicit content unless you already have what it takes.

Before we leave this, there are two final points to be made. The evolutionary story depends on the idea that only systems that work well will persist. But, first, systems will occur that do not persist. What of *their* contents? Second, in this context, working well means getting the right percepts constructed, and that clearly presupposes the notion of representational content.

Idealization and Infallibility

A number of pages ago, I promised to return to the question whether we can really assume that a cognitive system would be infallible under ideal conditions.

There are well-known philosophical reasons for resisting this assumption. If you take this line, you have to be prepared to *legislate* against alleged cases in which the truth differs from the result of ideal inquiry, and that means you have to adopt some form of verificationist anti-realism. You must, in short, be prepared to say that what isn't ideally detectable isn't *there*, and this looks more like arrogance than serious theory.

One needn't rely on this philosophical line of attack, however, for there is an uncontroversial empirical objection to the assumption. As we saw in our discussion of malfunction, error is the inevitable price of computational tractability. The *knowledge that mediates cognitive inferences is, of necessity, only typically and approximately true. Some bodies aren't rigid. Some rooms aren't square. Some noses *are* concave (see Gregory 1970). What is more, there is no idealizing away from this kind of error. If you want to consider a system with unlimited time and memory, you are going to be considering a system with a completely different functional architecture than the one that operates under real resource constraints.

When you take friction and air resistance away from a pendulum, you still have a pendulum. Furthermore, you have a pendulum whose period depends on its length in just the way in which period depends on length in "normal" pendulums. The independence of the effect of length on period from the effects of friction and air resistance is what makes it proper to idealize away from the latter. But when you reduce the resources required by an infallible program, what you typically get is not a program that performs acceptably but not optimally; what you typically get is a program that fails to perform at all, or one that performs very poorly. Typically, then, this infallible program (if there is one) is just a different program, root and branch, than the one that makes things tractable given limited resources by making simplifying assumptions. Computational work in early vision is a striking example of this general point. There are algorithms that will solve many of the computational problems infallibly, but they require unrealistic resources. Progress was made by turning to algorithms that rely on assumptions that, although they are fallible, hold quite generally in normal environments (Marr 1982; Ullman 1979).

Thus, the idea that one can idealize away from cognitive error is incompatible with a fundamental finding of the CTC. That theory holds all such idealizations to be fallacious on the ground that they violate the requirement that what one idealizes away from must be independent of what is left. According to the CTC, then, an ideal but finite cognitive system operating under ideal conditions will inevitably make lots of mistakes. Since L3 assumes the contrary, L3 is incompatible with the CTC.

Summary

It looks, tentatively, as if computationalists cannot understand mental representation in terms of covariation. In a way, we should have seen this coming: We're going to have covariance only when the epistemological conditions are right. Good epistemological conditions are ones that are going to get you correct (or at least rational) results. Conditions like that are bound to require semantic specification. Less obviously, but just as surely, covariance theories presupposes a kind of epistemological idealization that is forbidden by the CTC. In the next two chapters, we will see whether the most prominent contemporary variations on the basic Lockean theme manage to resolve these fundamental difficulties.

Chapter 5

Covariance II: Fodor

Jerry Fodor (1987) defends an account of the nature of mental representation that is remarkably similar to the one I have just discussed. The similarity is no accident; it will become clear as we go along that covariationists have a limited number of basic tools in the box. But there is no question that Fodor has added a few that are worth examining.

Background

Fodor begins by assuming the Representational Theory of Intentionality (which he calls the Representational Theory of Mind) and the Language-of-Thought Hypothesis (the hypothesis that mental representations are language-like symbols). Given these two assumptions, we can assume further that the problem of mental meaning generally reduces to the problem of understanding what it is for a primitive, nonlogical term of Mentalese to have a content. Given this focus, it will be convenient to have a convention for naming terms of Mentalese. In what follows, I shall write the term in Mentalese supposed to denote horses as |horse|; absolute values seem appropriate.

The basic idea—an idea Fodor calls the crude causal theory—is that symbol tokenings denote their causes and symbol types express the property whose instantiations reliably cause their tokenings.[1] Two problems immediately arise: that some noncats cause |cat|s, and that not all cats cause |cat|s.

The Disjunction Problem

Fodor calls the first problem the *disjunction problem,* for reasons that will emerge shortly. Suppose we try to describe a case of misrepresentation. A case of misrepresentation has to be a case like this: (1) Graycat causes a | dog | to occur in *S;* (2) | dog | expresses the property of being a dog in *S;* (3) Graycat is not a dog but a cat (of course). Now, since a cat (or, anyway, Graycat) causes a | dog | to occur in *S,* it follows that what | dog | must express in *S* is the property of being a dog-or-cat, or perhaps being a dog-or-Graycat, contrary to (2). It seems that any reason the crude causal theorist has to think that | dog | misrepresents Graycat as a dog is, for that theorist, a better reason to think that the content of | dog | has been misdescribed. Misrepresentation is always upstaged by a redescription of the alleged content. When the redescription is carried out, there is no misrepresentation. Hence, the crude causal theory implies that there is no misrepresentation.

It is tempting to reply that the causal route from Graycat to | dog | is not reliable. However, we can always make it reliable by describing the case in enough detail: There must be some situation in which Graycat reliably causes a | dog | in S—namely, the situation that obtained when, by hypothesis, Graycat was causally responsible for a | dog | in S. Moreover, there is such a thing as *systematic* misrepresentation: If I systematically misrepresent shrews as mice, this must be a case in which, according to the crude causal theory, shrews reliably cause | mouse |s in me. But there can't *be* such a case, since whatever is reliably caused by shrews is supposed to be a | shrew |.

Idealization

The obvious solution to the disjunction problem—one that Fodor himself briefly favored—is to idealize: In S | cat |s express the property of being a cat if, under ideal or optimal conditions, cats would reliably cause | cat |s in S. This move is, of course, familiar from our discussion of LOCKE, and it suffers from the same flaws: If the CTC is on the right track, there is no thoroughly naturalistic way to spell out the ideal conditions in question, and they won't eliminate error anyway.

Fodor in fact favors a different and far more ingenious solution.[2] The account pivots on the following claims: The fact that shrews sometimes cause |mouse|s in me depends on the fact that mice cause |mouse|s in me. On the other hand, the fact that mice cause |mouse|s in me doesn't depend on the fact that shrews sometimes cause |mouse|s in me. Mice look mousey to me, and that mousey look causes a |mouse|. But it is only because shrews also look mousey to me that shrews cause |mouse|s. Thus, if mice didn't cause |mouse|s, shrews wouldn't either. But it needn't work the other way; I could learn to distinguish shrews from mice, in which case mice would cause |mouse|s even though shrews would not.

This applies to the disjunction problem as follows; |mouse|s don't express the property of being a mouse-or-shrew, because the shrew-to-|mouse| connection is *asymmetrically dependent* on the mouse-to-|mouse| connection—the former connection would not exist but for the latter. In the case of genuinely disjunctive concepts, however, A-to-|D| connections are on a par with B-to-|D| connections, so |D|s express the property of being A-or-B.

Objections to Asymmetrical Dependence
I find this line unconvincing. Consider again the crucial counterfactuals:

> (i) If mice didn't cause |mouse|s, shrews wouldn't cause |mouse|s.

> (ii) If shrews didn't cause |mouse|s, mice wouldn't cause |mouse|s.

The alleged asymmetry depends on the claim that (i) is true and (ii) false. But is this really right? Shrews cause |mouse|s because they look like mice. Thus, if shrews didn't cause |mouse|s, that might be because (a) shrews didn't look like mice or because (b) mouse-looks didn't cause |mouse|s. If (b) were the culprit, though, mice wouldn't cause |mouse|s either, and that would make (ii) true.

It might seem that we can't blame (b) because the closest world in which shrews don't cause |mouse|s is the one in which (a) holds, not (b), since (b) requires a break in the rather central connection between mouse-looks and │mouse│s, whereas (a) requires only learning to distinguish mice and shrews. But this really isn't very persuasive. Perhaps shrews just look like mice to people, and finding out about shrews just makes them *uncertain* when they see either one. In a case like that, anything that will break the shrew-to-│mouse│ connection will break the mouse-to-│mouse│ connection as well. Even experts might perform randomly (perhaps the technology isn't adequate), even though they understand the difference perfectly well and can explain it to laypersons. Look what doctors do with diseases, or psychiatrists with psychoses and neuroses!

A variation on this theme suggests that the theory of asymmetrical dependence inverts the explanatory order: │mouse│s are wild when caused by shrews not because the more basic causal connection is with mice, but because │mouse│s express the property of being a mouse—something they might well do even if the dependence were symmetrical. Consider this story: In a certain tribe, all the youngsters are taught that they must catch a mouse for a certain potion the tribe needs. Mice are very rare, but only mice will do. Like all the other children, Broomhilda is taught how to catch a mouse (but not how to make the potion; only the medicine woman knows that). She is taught this by practicing on shrews. She has never seen a mouse, and she wouldn't recognize one if she saw one. Perhaps a mouse hasn't been seen in generations. Broomhilda knows there is a difference, however, for she knows at least this: Mice work in the potion, and shrews don't. Since the whole point of the training is to catch a mouse, the shrew-to-│S│ connection (│S│ is Broomhilda's internal representation) wouldn't exist but for the mouse-to-│S│ connection. │S│s are, as Millikan (1984) would say, reproduced in Broomhilda because of the connection with mice. But also, given the way things are learned, the connection between │S│s and mice wouldn't exist if it were not for the connection between shrews and │S│s. There is no saying which connection is more fundamental. Hence, the asymmetrical-dependence doctrine must hold that │S│ expresses the property of being a shrew-or-mouse. But it doesn't. It expresses the property of being a mouse, and *that* is why | S |s occasioned by shrews are wild.

A determined defender of asymmetrical dependence might avoid this criticism by claiming that scenarios like the ones just rehearsed that break down the asymmetry between (i) and (ii) are scenarios in which | mouse | (or | S |) is no longer a primitive term of Mentalese. But I don't think this will do, for it is pretty obvious that you can cook up similar scenarios for, say, | puce |.

Fodor's own reply is that the asymmetrical-dependence condition must apply *synchronically:* No matter how | mouse | and | shrew | are learned, current dispositions make the mouse-to-| mouse | connection primary. This strikes me as rather *ad hoc*, but let's see where it leads.

The picture Fodor has in mind is shown in figure 5.1. Mice cause mousey looks, which cause | mouse |s. Since shrews look mousey, they also cause mousey looks, thus poaching on the causal route from mice to | mouse |s and producing "wild" | mouse |s. Here are the relevant counterfactuals:

(1) If mice didn't cause | mouse |s, shrews wouldn't either. (T)

(2) If shrews didn't cause | mouse |s, mice wouldn't either. (F)

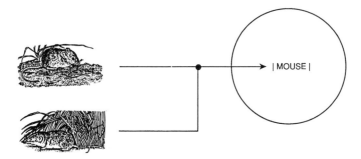

Figure 5.1
A shrew poaches on the mouse-to- | mouse | connection.

As indicated, we have the required asymmetrical dependence when (1) is true and (2) is false.

Start with (2). Figure 5.1 suggests two ways to break the shrew-to- | mouse | connection: (i) Mousey looks don't cause | mouse |s. But then mice won't cause | mouse |s either. Thus, (ii) shrews don't cause mousey looks. Perhaps shrews are extinct. More realistically, perhaps I come to *know something (perhaps tacitly) about how shrews and mice differ, and, as a result, shrews cease to even *look* like mice. But *mice* still look mousey, and hence they cause | mouse |s. So (2) is false, as desired.

Now consider (1). Again figure 5.1 suggests two ways to attack the mouse-to- | mouse | connection: (iii) Mousey looks don't cause | mouse |s. Since, by hypothesis, shrews poach by looking mousey, they will also cease to cause | mouse |s, and (1) is true, as required. Unfortunately, this way of making (1) true makes (2) true, as we just saw, so (iv) mice don't cause mousey looks. Perhaps mice become extinct, or acquire some disfiguring disease. But this won't affect the shrew-to- | mouse | connection, so (1) is false, contrary to requirements.

It looks as though the only way to have (1) true and (2) false is to employ different rules for evaluating them: Use (ii) to evaluate (2) and (iii) to evaluate (1). The possible worlds in which (1) is true and (2) is false are not the same possible worlds. To put it another way, there is no single interpretation that makes (1) true and (2) false. Therefore, (1) and (2) do not jointly express something about the connection between mice and shrews and that between mice and | mouse |s.

One might reply: "Well so what? All that means is that the definition of asymmetrical dependence is a bit messy. You have to say how (1) and (2) are to be (separately) evaluated." I wish I had a knock-down rebuttal to this reply, but I don't (even though I have the feeling there must be one). All I have is this: If you must get this tricky with the counterfactuals, you don't have a philosophical *explanation* any more; at best, you have a technically defensible equivalence between analysandum and analysans. It is hard to believe that the content of | r | is *mouse* rather than *mouse-or-shrew* BECAUSE if mice didn't cause ⅠmouseⅠs because mousey looks didn't then shrews wouldn't cause ⅠmouseⅠs either, and if shrews didn't cause ⅠmouseⅠs becauseshrews didn't look mousey then mice would still cause ⅠmouseⅠs (*ceteris paribus*, of course).

Maybe there *is* a way to make asymmetric dependence work without sacrificing explanation, but enough. As Fodor quite rightly says, the disjunction problem is the lesser of the two problems faced by the covariance theorist. Let's stop counting angels on pinheads and move on to where the action is.

Omniscience

The Crude Causal Theory says, in effect, that a symbol expresses a property if it's nomologically necessary that *all* and *only* instances of the property cause tokenings of the symbol. (Fodor 1987, p. 100)

Lots of cats never cause ⅠcatⅠs. (Well, to be safe, lots of rocks never cause ⅠrockⅠs. But I prefer to stick with the cat-and-mouse game.) But why is that a problem for the covariationist? The crude causal theory was expressed thus: ". . . symbol tokenings denote their causes, and the symbol types express the property whose instantiations reliably cause their tokenings." It isn't obvious that *this* says, in effect, that *all* instantiations of the property cause tokenings of the symbol. Wherefore this strong and bothersome *all*? Granted, some cats don't cause ⅠcatⅠs; but so what? Why isn't it enough that nothing else causes ⅠcatⅠs (or, rather, that nothing else causes ⅠcatⅠs in the basic way supposedly picked out by asymmetrical dependence)? It is well to get clear about this, because this seems to commit Fodor to the claim that cognitive systems are omniscient, and, as he admits, this is preposterous on its face. ". . . [P]roblems about the 'all' clause are, in my view," he writes, "very deep." So why is the 'all' clause *there*? Surprisingly, Fodor never answers this question, but the answer is quite simple: If some cats don't cause ⅠsⅠs, then it seems that the extension of ⅠsⅠ should be the subset of cats that *do* cause ⅠsⅠs. We need to rule out the possibility that ⅠsⅠ expresses the property of being, say, a black-and-white cat, or that of being Graycat. The only way the causal theorist can get around this is to insist on genuine covariation: All cats cause |s|s (or, anyway, any cat *would* cause an |s| *if given a fair chance*). But what is it to be *given a fair chance*?

The difficulty, of course, is that according to the CTC there is a fair chance that a cat will cause a |cat| only if the system is prepared to *attend* properly and to make the right *inferences* (or *inferences) on the basis of the right *knowledge*. But this sort of reply is clearly out of bounds; it will render the theory circular. Fodor realizes this but argues that, contrary to appearances, it *is* possible after all for a computationalist to specify causally sufficient conditions for a cat to cause a |cat|, or even for a proton to cause a |proton|, without trafficking in intentional or semantic notions.[3] Here is what he says:

> But though protons typically exert causal control over |proton|s via the activation of intentional mechanisms, a naturalistic semantics doesn't need to specify all that. All it needs is that the causal control should actually obtain, *however* it is mediated. The claim, to put it roughly but rather intuitively, is that it's sufficient for |proton| to express *proton* if there's a reliable correlation between protons and |proton|s, effected by a mechanism whose response is specific to psychophysical traces for which protons are *in fact* causally responsible. And that claim can be made in nonintentional, nonsemantic vocabulary. It just was.
>
> No doubt mechanisms that track nonobservables in the required way typically satisfy intentional characterizations (they're typically inferential) and semantic characterizations (they work because the inferences that they draw are sound). But that's OK because, on the one hand, the semantical/intentional properties of such mechanisms are, as it were, only contingently conditions for their success in tracking protons; and, on the other, what's required for |proton| to express *proton* is only that the tracking actually be successful. For purposes of semantic naturalization, *it's the existence of a reliable mind/world correlation that counts, not the mecha-*

nisms by which that correlation is effected.[4]   (Fodor 1987, pp. 121–122)

We have seen this move before; it is just the idea, scouted in the chapter 4 above, that the covariationist doesn't really owe us an account of the conditions under which, say, an *arbitrary* cat is guaranteed to produce a | cat |. All we need is (i) some guarantee that the relevant mechanism exists and (ii) a non-question-begging way to *pick out* that mechanism. The first part is plausible enough on general empirical grounds: There must be some circumstances in which cats are sufficient for | cat |s. And for Fodor the second is a cinch: "The mechanism that does the trick" does the trick! This is because all Fodor requires is a "naturalistic" way to pick out the mechanism, i.e., a way of picking out the mechanism without explicit use of intentional or semantic terms:

> What is required to relieve the worry that meaning will resist assimilation into the natural causal order is therefore, at a minimum, the framing of *naturalistic* conditions for representation. That is, what we want at a minimum is something of the form '*R represents S' is true if C* where the vocabulary in which condition C is couched contains neither intentional nor semantical expressions. (Fodor 1984a, p. 2)

Fodor says that avoiding semantical and intentional expressions is only a *minimal* requirement, but in fact he takes it to be sufficient:

> The reference to 'mechanisms of belief fixation' perhaps makes this look circular, but it's not. At least not so far. Remember that we're assuming a functional theory of believing (though not, of course, a functional theory of believing that p; . . . .). On this assumption, having a belief is just being in a state with a certain causal role, so—in principle at least—we can pick out the belief states of an organism without resorting to semantic or intentional vocabulary. But then it follows that we can pick out the organism's mechanisms of belief fixation without recourse to semantic or intentional vocabulary: The mechanisms of belief *fixation*

are, of course, the ones whose operations eventuate in the organism's having belief. (Fodor 1987, p. 105)

Perhaps we can pick out the mechanisms of belief fixation in "naturalistic" terms, but the CTC holds that we can't understand them or describe them without a healthy dose of representational lingo.

Well, admittedly, one philosopher's (or one scientist's) explanation is another's explanadum, but this seems like cheating to me. We are told that representation rests on a covariance between representation and representandum—between cats and | cats | s, for example. Covariance, in turn, is grounded in a mechanism that, under the right conditions, will produce a | cat | from a cat. According to the CTC, the mechanism in question can be understood only by appeal to inner representations, for the mechanism in question is one of inference from stored *knowledge. It follows that in order to understand the mechanism that the CTC invokes to explain the covariance between cats and | cat | s we must already understand representation and the explanatory role it plays in mental mechanisms. And that, by my lights, is enough to undermine the power of covariance theories to help us to understand the nature of representation in the CTC.

The problem, of course, is that it isn't enough to avoid intentional/semantic vocabulary; you must do it in a way that explains what representation is. It becomes obvious that just avoiding intentional/semantic vocabulary isn't enough when you see how easy it is. The problem, remember, was to say under what conditions cats are sufficient for | cat | s,[5] and to do it in naturalistic vocabulary. But look how easy it is: (i) Find an actual occasion in which a cat does cause a | cat |. Name that occasion O. (ii) Consider the mechanism that did the trick on occasion O (never mind how this worked, or whether it was peculiar to O), and call it M. (iii) Construct the desired counterfactual: Were M to operate on a cat in circumstances like those that obtained in O, a | cat | would result. Nothing to it!

The thing starts to come unraveled when we ask what O and M are like, for it is a fundamental consequence of the CTC that these must be *understood* inferentially (though, of course, they *can* be *picked out* naturalistically). The covariationist tells us that there is representation because there is covariance. The CTC tells us that there is covariance because there is representation, and Fodor agrees. But you can't have it both ways without undermining the explanatory power of one of the two doctrines. And since the philosophical problem before us is to explain representation in a way that will underwrite (not undermine) its explanatory role in the CTC, it is the covariationist doctrine that must go.

Here is a kind of analogy that may help clarify how I see the intellectual situation: Suppose someone tells you that the temperature of something depends on the amount of caloric in it. "What is caloric?" you ask. "Well," says your informant, "it is clear what one would like to say: Caloric is the stuff that increases in a thing when you raise its temperature. Of course, that's circular. But I can avoid the circle. Consider the mechanism that operates when you put tap water from the tap marked "C" in a pan on a lighted stove: Caloric is the stuff that mechanism causes to increase in the water." This identifies caloric without explaining it.

Idealization Again

We saw in chapter 4 that covariationists require idealization away from all sources of error. We are now in a position to put this point together with the point about circularity. The fact that you can't idealize away from error means that there is no *general* way to pick out a mechanism that will produce a |cat| in response to an arbitrary cat. Thus, the only way to do it is by reference to some *specific* instance or instances in which a cat *does* product a |cat|. We then say for all S that if S were in a situation like *that*, a cat would yield a |cat|. The sense that we no longer have an explanation of representation can be traced to the demonstrative. The account is essentially ostensive. "Representation," it says, "is when you have a case like *that*." Then you give an example or a sketch of what one would be like: "You know. It's like when you think there is a cat there because there *is* one there." There is no substantive way to specify the C in "In C, any cat would cause a cat in S," so the covariationist must, in the end, have recourse to ostension, and must hope you don't notice that there is no principled way to generalize on the example.

Chapter 6
Covariance III: Dretske

For present purposes, the account of the nature of representation as set out by Fred Dretske in his 1981 book *Knowledge and the Flow of Information* can be boiled down to the following two claims:

> (D1)   The semantic content of a cognitive state M is a privileged part of its informational content, *viz.*, that informational content of M which is nested in no other informational content of M.[1]

> (D2)   A cognitive state M of O has the proposition p as an informational content if the conditional probability that p is true, given that O is in M, is 1.

On this view, informational content is explicitly a matter of covariation between the representing state and the state represented.   Indeed, Dretske often glosses D2 as the claim that M is a perfect indicator of the truth value of p.   Perhaps it is worth emphasizing that, on this view, as on Fodor's and Locke's, M's covariation with p's holding isn't merely evidence that M has p as its informational content; it is constitutive: Representation *is* a special case of covariation on these accounts.

Misrepresentation
Notoriously, Dretske's account gives rise to difficulties in explaining the possibility of misrepresentation.   It follows from D2 that if p is the informational content of M, then p is true.   Hence, by D1, if p is the semantic content of M, p is true.   It looks as if there can't be a false representation.

Dretske is alive to this difficulty, and he seeks to get around it in what should by now be the familiar way: idealization. The crux of his maneuver as it is set out in *Knowledge and the Flow of Information* is to distinguish the "learning situation," when conditions are supposed to be optimal, from ordinary situations, when they are not. In the former case, the occurrence of a token of M in the system is a perfect indicator that p is true. The system thus comes to rely on the occurrence of tokens of M to infer that p is the case. (Or perhaps, in simple systems, occurrences of tokens of M simply assume the control functions appropriate to p's being true.) When conditions are not optimal, however, the indicator is no longer perfect: O can get into a token of state M even though p is not true. The inferential mechanism is still in place, however, so the organism infers that p is the case, contrary to fact.

The difficulties with this line of defense are well known.[2] First, only learned representations are covered, and a great deal is innate according to the CTC.[3] Second, there appears to be no noncircular way to distinguish the learning situation from others. On the face of it, organisms appear to learn to identify things without ever achieving perfection. I don't see how to get around this without simply stipulating that only situations in which an organization does develop a perfect indicator are to be counted as genuine learning situations. The danger of this move is that it runs a serious empirical risk: There is no reason to think there are any learning situations thus construed. Finally, it is hard to see how the occurrence of a token of M in O could be a perfect indicator that p is true if it is possible subsequently for a token of M to occur in O when p is false. What are we to say about what *would* have happened had one of these unfortunate circumstances obtained during the learning period? However this may be, it is certain that those tokens will not have p as an informational content and hence will not have p as a semantic content, so we are left without an account of misrepresentation.[4]

The fundamental source of these difficulties is the Lockean assumption that representation is essentially a matter of covariation. Since it is obvious that cognitive systems often misrepresent (i.e., often get into cognitive states that are not perfect indicators of the states of affairs they represent), cognitive representational content cannot be a species of informational content. The only way to save the idea in the face of this obvious fact is to attempt to define representational content in terms of informational content without making the former a species of the latter. There is really only one move that has a chance of working: The representational content of M is the informational content M would have under ideal conditions. And this is evidently the essence of Dretske's move (as it is of Fodor's and of the Lockean proto-theory discussed in chapter 4), except that Dretske implausibly holds that optimal conditions actually obtain during the "learning period." Idealization is forced on the covariationist by the obvious fact of misrepresentation, for misrepresentation is representation without covariation. Idealization is the only way to go with the idea that representation is covariation, for the covariationist, in the face of misrepresentation, *must* say, in effect, *"Well there would be covariation if things were nice."*

We have seen, however, that idealized covariance is problematic for the computationalist, for the CTC holds (i) that reliable mind-world covariation depends on representation, and not the other way around, and (ii) that it is not really possible to idealize away from error in any case. The theory of *Knowledge and the Flow of Information* doesn't help us with these fundamental problems.

Functional Meaning

Since the publication of *Knowledge and the Flow of Information,* Dretske has come up with what appears to be a different account of representation—an account specifically designed to deal with misrepresentation (Dretske 1986). This account identifies cognitive representation as a species of what Dretske calls functionally derived meaning:

> (M_f) d's being G means$_f$ that w is $F =_{df} d$'s function is to indicate the condition of w, and the way it performs this function is, in part, by indicating that w is F by its (d's) being G.

In the 1986 work, Dretske claims to be primarily concerned with

clarifying the appeal to functions in this analysis.[5] He emphasizes that the analysis itself is nothing particularly new and
different. If that is correct, then the line of criticism I have been
pressing against Lockean theories of representation should apply
to this analysis regardless of how the appeal to functions is
cashed out. Actually, a little work will reveal that Dretske's
analysis in "Misrepresentation" is a slight variation on themes
we have already rehearsed. The work is worth doing because it
helps us to see how the constraints operating on covariationist
theories always manage to push the advocates of covariation into
the same basic configurations.

At first blush, M_f looks unpromising because of the use of the
semantic term "indicate" on the right-hand side. One might well
complain that if we knew what it was for a cognitive state to
indicate something, we would already be home free. But this is
premature, for Dretske actually has in mind the relatively inno-
cent idea that d's being G indicates that w is F just in case d's being
G covaries with w's being F:

(M_f) d's being G means$_f$ that w is $F =_{df}$ d's function is to covary
with the condition of w, and the way it performs this function
is, in part, by d's being G when and only when w is F.

The appeal to functions in M_f does the same job it does in all
Lockean accounts. Not all covariance is representation; sunburns
don't represent overexposure to ultraviolet light, because it isn't
a *function* of sunburns to covary with overexposure to ultraviolet
light. If it is a *function* of d's being G to covary with w's being F,
then we have representation (meaning$_f$).

This allows for misrepresentation because d can fail to perform
its function. It is the function of a fuel gauge (let us suppose) to
indicate the amount of fuel in the tank. It has this function even
if the tank is full of water. When the tank is full of water, the gauge
misrepresents the tank as full of fuel.[6]

Evaluating M_f

There are two ways to understand M_f. Compare the following:

(i) There is something d whose function is to covary with (indicate) the state of the world; a state of d represents x iff it covaries with x under ideal conditions.[7]

(ii) A state M represents x iff it is the function of M to covary with x.

Let us call the second variation the *specific-function variation*, to emphasize that in it each representation is identified via a specific function. In contrast, the first variation is a general-function variation, because it requires only a blanket function claim to the effect that there is a something d whose function is to indicate the state of the world.

We needn't trouble further with the general-function variation, since that evidently leads us over ground already explored. Does the specific-function variation give us a genuine alternative to the general-function variations already considered?

In Millikan's (1984) hands it does; the result will be the subject of the next chapter. But in Dretske's hands, the specific-function route returns us to familiar Lockean territory. The crucial point is this: On Dretske's view, it is a necessary condition of its being R's function to covary with x that R would covary with x under normal (or optimal) conditions.[8] Idealized covariance is thus a necessary condition of meaning$_f$, and M_f thence inherits all the difficulties attendant on the idea that x represents y only if x would covary with y under ideal conditions.

Fixing Functions

I said above that Dretske is mainly concerned in "Misrepresentation" with the problem of clarifying the appeal to functions in M_f.[9] It is worth digressing to follow this line of thought because of what it reveals about the inner structure of the covariationist approach to representation. Here is the admirable illustration Dretske uses to introduce the problem:

> Some marine bacteria have internal magnets (called magnetosomes) that function like compass needles, aligning themselves (and, as a result, the bacteria) parallel to the earth's

magnetic field. Since these magnetic lines incline down-wards (toward geomagnetic north) in the northern hemisphere (upwards in the southern hemisphere), bacteria in the northern hemisphere, oriented by their magnetosomes, propel themselves toward geomagnetic north. The survival value of magnetotaxis (as the sensory mechanism is called) is not obvious, but it is reasonable to suppose that it functions so as to enable the bacteria to avoid surface water. Since these organisms are capable of living only in the absence of oxygen, movement towards geomagnetic north will take the bacteria away from oxygen-rich surface water and towards the comparatively oxygen-free sediment at the bottom. Southern hemispheric bacteria have their magnetosomes reversed, allowing them to swim toward geomagnetic south with the same beneficial results. Transplant a southern bacterium in the North Atlantic and it will destroy itself—swimming upwards (towards magnetic south) into the toxic, oxygen-rich surface water. (1986, p. 26)

According to M_f, if the orientation of the magnetosomes toward magnetic north is to mean$_f$ that oxygen-free water is in that direction, it must be the function of the magnetosomes to indicate the direction of oxygen-free water. The function clause in M_f is what identifies the representandum. But there seem to be several initially plausible ways to specify the function of the magnetosomes, and hence several initially plausible candidates for what is represented by the orientation of the magnetosomes. Hence are two choices:

Liberal   The function of the magnetosomes is to indicate the direction of oxygen-free water.

Conservative   The function of the magnetosomes is to indicate the direction of the surrounding magnetic field.

On the liberal reading, hemispherically transplanted bacteria are victims of misrepresentation; on the conservative reading they are not. On the conservative reading, even bar magnets don't fool them. Indeed, on the conservative reading, the only thing that could fool the bacterium would be a loss of polarity in the magnetosomes themselves, or some mechanical hindrance to their changing orientation. This raises the possibility that one can turn every case of misrepresentation into a case of the proper representation of something else simply by taking a more conservative view of the relevant functions.

In order to prevent this sort of deflationary trivialization of M_f, Dretske thinks he is obliged to find a way to rule out conservative construals of function in favor of liberal construals in every case in which misrepresentation is clearly possible. Only on the liberal reading can we say, for example, that in hemispherically transplanted bacteria the magnetosomes fail to perform their function—their function is to indicate the direction of oxygen-free water, they fail, and the organism destroys itself.

Dretske claims that a liberal reading is motivated only when the system exhibits a certain degree of complexity, a degree of complexity that magnetotaxic bacteria plausibly lack. The idea is relatively simple. Suppose we have two detection mechanisms that operate in parallel: the magnetosomes (as before) and a temperature sensor. Since surface water is generally warmer, an organism that prefers colder to warmer water will generally avoid oxygen-rich surface water. Imagine, further, some internal device R that changes the organism's direction of locomotion in response to either a change in the orientation of the magnetosomes or a change in the temperature sensor. The magnetosomes represent the direction of the magnetic field; the temperature sensor represents changes in temperature. What does R represent? According to Dretske, it represents the direction of oxygen-free water. No more proximal (conservative) representandum will do, according to Dretske, because the state of R never—even under optimal conditions—means$_n$ anything less distal than something about the direction of oxygen-free water.

Our problem with the bacteria was to find a way of having the orientation of its magnetosomes mean$_f$ that oxygen-free water was in a certain direction without arbitrarily dismissing the possibility of its meaning$_f$ that the magnetic field was aligned in that direction. We can now see that with the multiple resources described . . . this possibility can be non-arbitrarily dismissed. *R cannot* mean$_f$ that [the temperature is changing] or [that the state of the temperature sensor is changing], because it doesn't, even under optimal conditions, mean$_n$ this.[10] (1986, p. 34)

Even this will not be enough if, as Dretske points out, we are prepared to tolerate disjunctive meanings and say that R means$_f$ that magnetosome orientation or temperature-sensor change has occurred. However, if the system can be classically conditioned, so that any proximal stimulus s_1 could come to substitute for (say) magnetosome orientation, then there is no definite disjunction of proximal stimuli to fall back upon. Throughout the system's conditioning history, different proximal stimuli will mediate the detection of F. "Therefore," Dretske writes,

> if we are to think of these cognitive mechanisms as having a time-invariant function at all (something that is implied by their continued—indeed, as a result of learning, more efficient—servicing of the associated need), then we *must* think of their function, not as indicating the nature of the proximal (even distal) conditions that trigger positive responses . . . but as indicating the condition F for which these diverse stimuli are signs. (1986, pp. 35–36)

This whole exercise is curious. Dretske is worried that misrepresentation will be ruled out by deflationary conservative function assignments. Thus, he needs to motivate

A function of F is to indicate *x*

in cases in which R doesn't indicate *x*. The passage above makes it clear that Dretske accepts the following constraint on the relevant function assignments:

A function of R is to indicate *x* only if R would covary with *x* under optimal conditions.

This is what does all the work in the arguments; deflationary conservative attributions of content are ruled out solely on the ground that the relevant covariance wouldn't hold "even under optimal conditions." The appeal to functions is completely idle here. It isn't that conservatives are wrong about *functions;* we can spell out their mistake—the mistake Dretske attributes to them, anyway—in the language of covariance without mentioning functions at all.

It is no surprise that, for Dretske, representation is where the covariance is. If you find covariance with a distal feature, not with a proximal one, then of course it is the distal feature that is represented. Dretske's point is that sufficiently complex systems can get into states that covary (ideally) with distal features but not with proximal ones, and hence that covariationists can deal with a deflationary conservative who tries to undermine the theory by systematically substituting correct representation of the more proximal for misrepresentation of the more distal.

Progress is progress, and one shouldn't knock it. Still, it is important to realize that blocking the deflationary conservative does nothing toward explaining idealized covariance in terms that do not beg the questions. Nor does it help with the disjunction problem, the problem that notoriously bedevils the account in *Knowledge and the Flow of Information.* That problem applies with full force to the doctrine of "Misrepresentation." Suppose that both mice and shrews cause (covary with) | *M* |s. Can | *M* |s be | mouse |s? That depends on whether a function of | *M* | s is to covary with mice but not with shrews. How are we to tell? Disappointingly, the only help "Misrepresentation" gives us with this question is to tell us how to use covariance to rule out function attributions. It is not a function of | *M* |s to covary with shrews if | *M* | wouldn't covary with shrews under ideal conditions. We are thus led right back into the familiar territory we have already explored.[11]

There is a glimmer of an idea here, though: Perhaps representation can be explained in terms of function, and functions can be explained without recourse to idealized covariance or to any other tacitly (or explicitly) intentional or semantic concepts. That is Millikan's strategy, the subject of the next chapter.

Chapter 7
Adaptational Role

Exposition

In an important series of publications, Ruth Millikan has offered a subtle and complex account of representation in terms of the adaptational role of symbols and the adaptational roles of the mechanisms that produce them and respond to ("interpret") them. (See especially Millikan 1984, 1986; see also Papineau 1984.) Millikan's treatment resists easy summary: I cannot, in the course of a single chapter, hope to do full justice to the theory. Instead, I will concentrate on the basics, illustrated in connection with what Millikan takes to be the most fundamental type of case. My purpose, as in my chapters on Fodor and Dretske, is the limited one of giving enough of the flavor of the theory to determine whether it is suitable as an explication of the concept of representation appealed to in the CTC.[1]

Here is the fundamental formulation:

(M1) C is a truth condition for r in $S =_{df} C$'s obtaining is a *basic factor* in a Normal Case for the performance of the Proper Functions of r- interpreters.[2]

Something x performs a Proper Function in a system S when it does the sort of thing the doing of which has been, historically, responsible for the replication of things of x's type.[3] Thus, circulation of the blood is a Proper Function of hearts because it is the fact that hearts contribute to blood circulation in the way they do that has been, historically, responsible for the replication of hearts, and hence for the historical persistence of that type of organ.[4]

A basic factor[5] for the performance of a Proper Function is a factor that tracks the selective importance of the Normal Case of that function fulfilling its Proper Function.[6] A Normal Case is one in which the function is performed *successfully*—i.e., a case in which the item in question does its stuff and everything else conspires to produce the kind of result that is responsible for that item's replication.

Millikan's suggestive illustration is the bee dance. When a bee dance is performed properly, it has a certain *orientation*. A consequence of a properly performed bee dance is that spectator bees fly off in a direction that corresponds to the orientation of the dance. But the whole business is a *success* (i.e., comes off in the way that accounts for the replication of the relevant mechanisms) only if the bees find flowers in that direction (hence find pollen, hence produce nectar, hence honey, hence food, hence the means of survival). So a Normal Case—which need not be the *usual* case at all—is a case in which spectators respond to a dance by flying off in the direction that corresponds to the dance's orientation and find flowers as a result. Flowers' being in the relevant direction is, therefore, a *basic factor* for the dance interpreter's functioning Properly in response to a dance: no flowers, no pollen; no pollen, no food; no food, no reinforcement (via natural selection) for the mechanisms that respond to bee dances.

At first glance, it might seem that the Normal Case is loaded with *basic factors*: There has to be enough light, the wind can't be blowing too hard, the flowers can't be deadly to bees, there can't be bee predators or clouds of DDT in the relevant direction, and so on. What, one might wonder, makes it the case that the content of the bee dance is *flowers in the o-direction* (i.e., flowers in the direction corresponding to the orientation of the dance) rather than, say, *no predators in the o-direction*?

The answer is that the o-direction's being a predator-free zone is not part of the content of a bee dance because it is not basic to the Normal Case; rather, it is part of the background or boundary conditions of such cases.[7] In Normal Cases there are no predators, no nuclear wars, no hurricanes, no poisonous flowers, and so forth, and there is plenty of light and air, the earth moves in the usual way relative to the sun, etc. But although these are all necessary conditions for Normal interpreter performance, they are not basic factors; flower presence in the o-direction is the (or a) basic factor.

What makes the presence of flowers in the o-direction a basic factor, and the presence of light and the absence of predators a background condition? The idea is that it is the presence of flowers, and not the absence of predators, that tracks the selective significance of Normal Cases of bee-dance-interpreter function. Although this is clear enough intuitively, the notion of *basic factors* operative here has application outside of a selectionist framework. I will digress briefly to indicate what this application is because it has some independent interest, and because seeing it at work in a nonselectionist context helps to clarify what is going on in the selectionist contexts that are central to Millikan's account.

Basic Factors
Consider the simple pendulum law:

$$2\pi\sqrt{l/g} = T$$

This is an idealization; it captures only the contribution of length and gravity to period, ignoring friction and air resistance. It works because of two facts. First, length and gravity are independent of friction and air resistance; g and l don't change as a function of friction or air resistance. The idealization represented by equation 7.1 wouldn't work if increasing the friction shortened the length. Second, length and gravity are "basic factors" in this situation: One can begin with equation 7.1 and superimpose the effects of friction and air resistance, but one cannot begin with the contribution of friction and air resistance to period and then superimpose the contribution of length and gravity. *There is no such thing as the way a pendulum would behave were length not a factor, whereas there is such a thing as the way a pendulum would behave were air resistance and friction not factors.* Experimentally, the point is that it makes sense to reduce friction and air resistance and note whether the period beings to approximate

$2\pi\sqrt{l/g}$; we cannot manipulate length and note whether the period begins to approximate what it would be if friction, air resistance, and gravity were the only factors, for there is nothing to approximate.

The Normal Case for the functioning of the bee-dance interpreter is supposed to be an idealization in the same sense in which the simple pendulum law is an idealization: It focuses on the basic factors—the factors responsible for the basic phenomenon—and it ignores factors not constitutive of that basic phenomenon. In the Normal Case, the spectators react to the dance by flying off in the direction of the dance orientation. They find flowers. They gather pollen. They return to the hive and make honey. We don't mention the fact that clouds of DDT are not encountered, the fact that the wind doesn't blow them off course, that night doesn't fall, that the distance isn't so great that they drop from exhaustion, and so on, and so on. These are all relevant factors, but they aren't basic; they don't *ground* the phenomenon. There is an asymmetry between the role played by the flowers and that played by the absence of DDT. Although both are necessary conditions for success, the dance interpreter doesn't get replicated because of the cases in which spectators fail to encounter DDT, for there were presumably lots of such cases in which there were no flowers. Hence, "Spectators respond to the dance by flying off in the direction of the dance orientation, where they find no DDT and hence survive" does not describe a Normal Case in a way that specifies what makes Normal Cases of dance-interpreter function *Normal*.[8]

It is interesting to examine how Millikan's theory treats the case of the magnetotaxic bacteria discussed by Dretske. The problem, recall, is how to arbitrate between the liberal and conservative construals of the representational significance of magnetosome orientation. Liberals hold that the function of magnetosome orientation is to indicate the direction of safe water; conservatives hold that its function is to indicate the orientation of the magnetic field.

Millikan's theory comes down squarely on the side of liberalism, for the Normal Case is surely the case in which the locomotion mechanisms respond to magnetosome movement by propelling the organism away from the surface to safe (oxygen-free) water. Hence, the relevant *basic factor* is the presence of safe water in the o-direction (*viz.* down, toward geomagnetic north), for it is the role played by the interpreter—the locomotion mechanism, in this case—in getting the organism to safe water that is responsible for the replication of the interpreter (the locomotion mechanisms).

But why not say "The magnetosome indicates the direction of magnetic north, and the interpreter acts on the rule *Safe water in the direction of magnetic north*"? Because magnetic north's being in the o-direction is not a basic factor in the interpreter's (the locomotion system's) performing its function of getting the organism to safe water.[9] The interpreter was replicated because, in the Normal Case, it responded to magnetosome orientation in a way that led the organism down to safe water, not because it led the organism in the direction of magnetic north. From the point of view of selection, the fundamental connection is the one between magnetosome orientation and the direction of safe water, and it is the interpreter's role in mediating that connection that has led to to its replication.[10]

Evaluation

Despite the considerable merits of Millikan's account, it will not do as an account of the concept of representation required by the CTC. The reason is simple: The CTC is committed to an ahistorical notion of representation, and Millikan's notion is essentially historical.

Duplicates
Imagine a kind of duplicating machine that duplicates organisms—not by cloning, or by any other biochemical process that uses the information coded in the organism's DNA, but just as a copy machine duplicates a printed page without understanding it. The machine I have in mind produces a perfect physical duplicate of an organism without "understanding it." The "transporter" familiar to fans of *Star Trek* is presumably such a device,

although it destroys the original in the process of producing a duplicate in another place. Will a duplicate of an organism have the same representations as the original? The intuition is fairly widespread that it will. Indeed, the assumption behind the *Star Trek* transporter is that the duplicate is the same person who entered the transporter. There seems little doubt that, for the purposes of a psychology experiment, a molecule-by-molecule duplicate of a person would do as well as the original. To deny this seems to be to deny physicalism. (See the example attributed to Block by Fodor [1987, p. 40].)

The CTC goes farther than simple physicalism; it asserts that, in order to preserve the identity of a cognitive system (if not a whole mind or person), it suffices to produce a computational duplicate. Two systems running the same program on the same data structures are, according to the CTC, cognitively indistinguishable. Since physical duplicates are bound to be computational duplicates, the idea that physical duplicates must share cognitive states is a consequence of CTC. Computationalism holds that cognitive systems are automatic formal systems. It follows that any two automations of the same form system are the same cognitive system. However, a perfect physical duplicate of D will automate a formal system F if and only if D automates F.

An exactly parallel argument will work for any theory that holds that a cognitive system can be specified in a way that abstracts from its physical realization (e.g., connectionist theories), for to abstract from physical realization is to abstract from the history of those realizations. Current ahistorical state, according to this approach, determines current cognitive capacities, and hence must determine current representational content. The CTC abstracts from history for the same reason it abstracts from the actual items in a system's current environment: For better or worse, the CTC seeks a theory of cognitive capacities of the sort that might be brought to bear on radically different environments (with differing success, no doubt), and that might be realized in radically different stuff.

A conspicuous feature of Millikan's account is that perfect

physical duplicates need not have the same representations. This is an immediate consequence of the fact that representational content is essentially a matter of *history* on Millikan's view. A perfect physical duplicate of me will have no evolutionary history or learning history at all. It will make no sense to ask of any of the mechanisms or subsystems of such a duplicate what factors were responsible for their replication: they weren't replicated in the sense required by Millikan's account.

It follows immediately that Millikan's account cannot be imported to explicate representation as that concept figures as an explanatory construct in computationalist theories of cognition. To put it crudely: According to computationalist accounts, history is an accidental property of a cognitive mechanism. According to computationalism, cognitive systems are individuated by their computational properties, and these are independent of history.

Someone with Millikanite leanings might be tempted to say that duplicate is cognitively equivalent to its original on the ground that it duplicates something with the right history. But this, in fact, amounts to abandoning the Millikan approach at a very fundamental level, for it amounts to conceding that it is really current state, ahistorically conceived, that underwrites cognitive content. What duplication produces, after all, is something that satisfies the same molecular blueprint as the original. If that is enough to ensure cognitive equivalence, then the significance of the original's history can only be that it resulted in an organism with the right molecular blueprint. History ceases to be of the essence, lapsing into the role of the only available technology for producing, without a prototype to copy, a system with the right molecular structure.

Another desperate attempt to somehow capitalize on Millikan's theory in order to give an account of representation that is consistent with computationalism is to think of the relevant history as somehow imminent in synchronically specified computational states. According to this idea, only when we think of the current state of a system as the product of a certain possible history does it make sense to characterize that system representationally. Although I think this idea has some merit of its own,[11] it is certainly no variation on Millikan, for it will surely be possible to describe various different histories that might have led to the same molecular blueprint or computational architecture—histories that will license quite different content attributions.[12] On Millikan's view, the point of appealing to actual history is to eliminate this kind of ambiguity (or indeterminacy, if you like); *actual* history determines the real content from among the possible ones.

A slightly more interesting possibility is that a physical duplicate would share the original's representations on the ground that selectionist/adaptationist explanations of the mechanisms in the original do carry over to the duplicate. The idea would be to claim, for example, that my duplicate's heart has the same Proper Functions as mine on the grounds that (i) the duplicate system is the way it is because *mine* is the way it is and (ii) my heart *does* have blood circulation as a Proper Function.

There is a good deal to be said for this suggestion (which I owe to Clayton Lewis). After all, genetic replication mechanisms are no more sensitive to selection history than the *Star Trek* transporter. Both mechanisms simply take things as they find them and replicate them, not on the basis of functional properties, but on the basis of physical properties on which functional properties supervene. It is hard to see, therefore, how to tell a story that will allow genetic replication to preserve Proper Functions but will not allow transporter replication to preserve them as well.[13]

Plausible as this line is, it won't help prop up a Millikanite reading of representation in the CTC. To repeat, the crucial issue is whether representation is grounded in the current state of the system, regardless of the history of that system. And on that issue the CTC is absolutely unambiguous: Computationally equivalent states are representationally equivalent. Yet computationally equivalent states need share no historical properties at all. From a computational perspective, historical properties are accidental properties. This is why computationalists can coherently hope to bypass the learning process. The CTC entails that if we *give* a system the same data structures that a natural system must acquire by learning, then (barring differences in computational architecture) we have a cognitively equivalent system. No computationalist can consistently suppose that a system that knows English must have *learned* it. And what goes for learning obviously goes for evolution as well. It is which data structures you have, not how you got them, that counts. Without this assumption, AI makes no sense at all.[14] No account that (like Millikan's) takes the history of a data structure seriously can be right for the CTC.

History and Belief
It is worth digressing a moment to point out that beliefs *are* individuated in a way that is sensitive to history. To borrow an example from Stich (1983), the belief my duplicate expresses with the words "I sold my car for a thousand dollars" is false because he didn't own the car in question, whereas the belief I express with the same words is true. We therefore have different beliefs, though by hypothesis we are computationally (indeed physically) equivalent. The problem is that my duplicate never acquired title to the car in question; I did. Hence, history matters to belief contents. If you are interested in belief contents, then you will do well to formulate an account that is sensitive to historical properties.

It doesn't follow from this, of course, that *representation* is sensitive to historical properties. In fact, nearly the opposite follows: Since data structures aren't sensitive to historical properties, it follows that beliefs aren't data structures. Moreover, it follows that beliefs don't inherit their contents from constituent data structures, as the RTI claims. This is one reason why philosophers who are interested in the semantics of belief (and of 'believes') are bound to misrepresent representation in the CTC: Data structures are insensitive to all sorts of things—such as historical properties—to which beliefs (and the other propositional attitudes) are exquisitely tuned. There is a good reason for this. As Stich points out, the CTC doesn't want to explain why my duplicate can't sell my car. Or, to put it as Ned Block does (in the example cited by Fodor, quoted above), some differences in belief are not legitimate sources of psychological variance.

content *rocks in the direction of the dance orientation*, even though we would be mystified about the evolutionary significance of the whole business. It seems pretty clear that speculation about the evolutionary history (and even learning history) of central cognitive mechanisms will be possible only after we have a pretty good idea what representations are actually required. I don't see how we can hope to understand the adaptational significance of the abstract functional architecture of the brain until we know what cognitive capacities it underwrites. But to know that, we must traffic heavily in mental representation. Epistemologically, then, representation is prior to adaptational role. Moreover, and much more important, the explanatory order follows the epistemological order in this case. We can't explain the adaptational role of a cognitive capacity without presupposing mental representation, for a capacity is *cognitive* (and the particular cognitive capacity it is) only in virtue of its semantic characterization.

Those who hope to explain representation in terms of adaptational role, then, face a dilemma reminiscent of that faced by the Lockean covariance theorist. The adaptational significance of brain mechanisms is surely tracked by their cognitive significance to a large extent. If one wants to explain the adaptational significance of the brain, then, one must be in a position to specify the cognitive architecture of the brain. The adaptational significance of the brain presupposes its cognitive capacities, and (according to the CTC, at least) cognitive capacities rest on representational capacities. This order of explanation is undermined if representation is explained (defined) in terms of adaptational role. Hence the following dilemma: If one wants to explain (define) representation in terms of adaptational role, one cannot also explain the adaptational role of brain mechanisms in terms of its representational capacities, as the CTC proposes to do.

Conclusion

Millikan's theory is sophisticated and complex. I l
ignore most of the sophistication and complexity, for
from my main concern here, which is to discover wh
tation must be if the CTC is to be true and explanatoi
entails that history is irrelevant to content, and Milli
says that history is the very essence of the thing. This
on Millikan; she was after intentionality (belief, etc.
sentation in the CTC.

The Evidential Value of Adaptational Role

Before going on to other possibilities, however, we
note of a final point. When I introduced covarianc
chapter 1, I suggested that one might be move
representation in covariance because one discovers
neural structure is an edge detector by noticing that
and only when there is an edge in the organism's
Obviously, an adequate treatment of representatic
count for the evidential role of covariance. Should
that an adequate treatment of representation acc
evidential role of selective history?

The problem with this suggestion is that we sel
selective history of anything. Or, rather, we seldom
edge of selective history that is epistemologically pr
facts about function and representation we are
establishing. We don't begin with the selective hist
dance mechanisms and then infer the content of b
exploit covariance to infer a probable content and th
the selective history. Of course, the availability
reconstruction in a case of this kind is powerful
The discovery that bees find flowers when they fly
to bee dances, together with our knowledge that th
flowers, leaves us feeling satisfied that the content
flowers in the direction of the dance orientation. Nev
always happened that spectator bees flew off in t
the dance orientation, found a pile of rocks, mille
went home, we would, I think, be justified in

Chapter 8
Interpretational Semantics

Summary and Advertisement

A central insight of the seventeenth century was that mental meaning cannot be understood in terms of resemblance. If the semantic relations between mind and world cannot be understood on the hypothesis that the mind is *like* the world, literally sharing properties with the things it represents, how can it be understood? In the hands of Locke and his successors, covariance replaced resemblance. But whatever advantages this had for Locke, mental representation cannot be understood in terms of covariation by those who want to follow the CTC in supposing that mental representation *explains* how systems manage to get into states that covary with the states of the world. And the attempt to understand mental representation in terms of adaptational roles also appears to reverse the explanatory order central to the CTC, and to be inconsistent with the thesis that cognition (and hence representation) supervenes on abstract formal structure that need not be historically specified.

What is next? The demise of similarity, idealized covariance, and adaptationist theories leaves us with only one candidate: functional role. The approach I will sketch in this chapter— "Interpretational Semantics"—turns out to be ontologically equivalent to a kind of functional-role semantics. However, Interpretational Semantics has, to my intellectual palate, a very different flavor than functional-role semantics; it is motivated in a very different way than typical functional-role theories, it directs our attention to quite different issues, and it generates a different dialectic. These virtues, I think, swamp the significance of the underlying ontological equivalence I will eventually notice in the next chapter.

Interpretational Semantics is really not an alternative to the traditional theories, which are best construed as answers to a different question. Interpretational Semantics is an account of representation in the CTC, whereas most philosophical discussion of mental representation has to do with Intentionality—i.e., with the contents of thoughts—rather than with the contents of the representations of a computational system. The theory I called the Representational Theory of Intentionality in chapter 2 would forge a tight link between representation and intentionality. But this, as we will see in chapter 10, is extremely problematic if we accept the CTC and the Interpretational Semantics that (I claim) inevitably goes with it. The kind of meaning required by the CTC is, I think, not Intentional Content anymore than entropy is history. There is a connection, of course, but at bottom representation in the CTC is very different from intentionality. To keep this point in the foreground, I will eventually introduce the special term *s-representation* (for simulation-based representation) to stand for the kind of representation described below. The thesis of Interpretational Semantics is that s-representation is the kind of representation the CTC requires to ground its explanatory appeals to representation.

It seems clear that if we are going to understand what representation is in the CTC, we should begin by understanding clearly what it does, and how. Representation is an explanatory construct in the CTC. Until we understand its explanatory role in that framework, we have no serious chance of understanding how it should be grounded for that framework. In order to get a clear picture of how the CTC proposes to exploit representation in the explanation of cognition, it is essential that we also gain a clear picture of the role of computation, for the main thesis of the CTC is that cognitive systems cognize by computing representations. The concepts of representation and computation are correlative in CTC and must be understood together.

Explaining Addition

The CTC proposes to explain cognitive capacities by appeal to representation and computation in exactly the way that arithmetical capacities of calculators (such as addition) are standardly explained by appeal to representation and computation. The main explanatory strength of the CTC is that it proposes to explain cognition in terms of antecedently understood notions of representation and computation—notions the CTC takes to be unproblematic in a variety of familiar noncognitive contexts such as calculating and elementary computer programming. We would do well to begin, then, by reviewing the "received" explanation of addition in adding machines.

To add is to be described by the plus function, $+(\langle m, n\rangle)= s$. Hence, to explain what makes a system an adder is to explain the fact that the system is described by $+$. But $+$ is a function whose arguments and values are numbers; and whatever numbers are, they are not states or processes or events in any physical system. How, then, can a physical system be described by $+$? How can a physical system traffic in numbers and hence add? The answer, of course, is that *numerals*—i.e., representations of numbers—can be states of a physical system, even if the numbers themselves cannot. A physical system adds by trafficking in numerals and hence, indirectly, in the numbers those numerals represent.

The input to a typical adding machine is a sequence of button pressings: $\langle C, M, +, N, =\rangle$, i.e., $\langle clear,\ first\ addend,\ plus,\ second\ addend,\ equals\rangle$. The output is a display state, D, which is a numeral representing the sum of the two addends. We may think of the button-pressing sequences as arguments to a function g that gives display states as values. An adding machine *satisfies g*; that is, the arguments and values of g are literally states of the physical system.[1] Addition, as was remarked above, relates numbers, not physical states of some machine, so a physical system cannot literally satisfy the plus function. What an adding machine does is *instantiate* the plus function. It *instantiates* addition by *satisfying* the function g whose arguments and values represent the arguments and values of the addition function, or in other words, have those arguments and values as interpretations.

Putting all this together, we have that something is an adding machine because

1. we can interpret button pressings (or the internal states they cause) as numbers,[2]

2. we can interpret displays (or the internal states that cause them) as numbers.

3. the device causally associates sequences of button pressings with displays (i.e., it satisfies a button-pressing-to-display function),

and, given all this,

4. if a token of the button-pressing events interpreted as n and m were to occur, then a token display event interpreted as $n+m$ would normally occur as a consequence. The device instantiates the addition function by satisfying the function mentioned in step 3, for that function is interpretable as the addition function.

To get a physical device to add, you have to get it to satisfy a function interpretable as addition. And that means you have to design it so that getting it to represent a pair of addends causes it to represent their sum.

The following is a useful picture of this whole conception of adding machines. I call it the Tower Bridge picture because it reminds me of London's Tower Bridge.

$$+: I(\langle\langle C, N, +, M, =\rangle\rangle) = \langle\, n, m\,\rangle \longrightarrow I\,(D) = n + m$$

$$I \qquad\qquad\qquad\qquad\qquad I$$

$$g: \langle\, C, N, +, M, =\rangle == \text{(computation)} ===D ====\!\!\!\Longrightarrow$$

The top span pictures the function instantiated: +, in our present case. It takes a pair of numbers onto their sum. The bottom span corresponds to the function satisfied (called simply g). It takes a quintuple of button pressings onto a display. The vertical arrows correspond to interpretation: $I(\langle C, N, +, M, =\rangle)$ is the interpretation of $(\langle C, N, +, M, =\rangle)$, namely $\langle n, m\rangle$, the pair of numbers represented by N and M. $I(D)$ is the interpretation of the display, which will be the sum of n and m if the thing works right. Under interpretation, the bottom span is revealed as an instantiation of the top span; computation is revealed as addition.

Computation

We have reduced the problem of explaining addition to the problem of explaining why the machine satisfies g, the function that instantiates addition. In standard adding machines, the values of g are *computed* from the corresponding arguments; adding machines add by computing the appropriate representations.

Of course, functions need not be computed to be satisfied. Set mousetraps satisfy a function from trippings to snappings without computing it, and physical objects of all kinds satisfy mechanical functions without computing them. The planets stay in their orbits without computing them. Missiles, on the other hand, compute their trajectories (sometimes), and, in general, complex systems often satisfy functions by computing them. Humans, in particular, routinely satisfy functions by computing them. This is how recipes and instruction manuals enable you to satisfy functions you don't know how to satisfy directly. The recipe for hollandaise sauce, for example, specifies such things as eggs and double boilers as inputs and hollandaise sauce as output. When you execute such a recipe, you satisfy a function having the recipe inputs as arguments and the hollandaise (the recipe output) as value. Recipes analyze such functions into simple functions you know how to satisfy directly—e.g., add three eggs to the contents of the bowl.[3]

To compute a function g is to execute a program that gives o as its output on input i just in case $g(i) = o$. Computing reduces to program execution, so our problem reduces to explaining what it is to execute a program.

The obvious strategy is to exploit the idea that program execution involves *steps*, and to treat each elementary step as a function that the executing system simply *satisfies*. To execute a program is to satisfy the steps.

But what guarantees that the steps are executed—i.e., satisfied—"in the right order"? Program execution is surely disciplined step satisfaction. Where does the discipline come in? The discipline takes care of itself. Functions satisfied by d specify causal connections between events in d, so if d satisfies f and g and if the current value of f is an argument for g, then an execution of the f step will produce an execution of the g step. Program execution reduces to step satisfaction.[4]

You won't go far wrong if you think of it this way. Imagine the program expressed as a flow chart. Each box in the chart represents a step. To execute a step is to satisfy its characteristic function, i.e., the function specified by the input/output properties of the box. If you think of the arrows between the boxes as causal arrows, the result is a causal network with steps (i.e., functions to be satisfied) at the nodes. A system executes the program if that causal network gives the (or a) causal structure of the system.[5]

The Role of Representation in This Explanation

The arguments and values of the button-pressing-to-display function that play the role of representations—i.e., the button-pressing sequences and the display states themselves—need not be symbols with any use or meaning outside the system that computes them. What matters is only that the system satisfy a function g that instantiates +. That is, there must exist an interpretation I such that

$$g(x) = y \quad \text{iff} \quad +(I(x)) = I(y).$$

It is, in short, simply the fact that g is isomorphic to + that makes the arguments and values of g representations of numbers for a system that satisfies g. It is sufficient for the arguments and values of g's being representations of addends and sums that there exist an interpretation mapping g onto +: The arguments and values of g's being representations of numbers is *constituted* by the fact that g instantiates +; representation is just a name for the relation induced by the interpretation mapping between the elements of g and the elements of +.

That there is no "further fact"[6] to representation in this case beyond g's instantiating + is obscured by the use of symbols with a meaning that is independent of their use in the system. One is tempted to suppose that the display state that looks like "5" would mean five regardless of whether g actually instantiates +. And so it would—*to us*. But its meaning in the system might be something quite different. To see this, we simply have to imagine that the buttons are mislabeled and that the display wires are crossed. In such a case we would have to discover what represented what, and this we would do by establishing a mapping, I, between g and + such that

$$g(x) = y \quad \text{iff} \quad +(I(x)) = I(y).$$

Indeed, it suffices to notice that it *makes sense* to suppose that the buttons *could* be mislabeled, or that the display wires *could* be scrambled, for this would make no sense if the meanings of input and output states were determined by the conventional meanings of those states considered as symbol tokens. We say that a display is scrambled because the conventional meanings of the display don't match the meanings that they have in the system, and this evidently requires that displays have a meaning in the system that is independent of their conventional meanings.

We are now in a position to see that it is somewhat misleading to speak of the explanatory role of representation in this context. The explanatory burden is carried by the fact of simulation and the correlative concept of interpretation. There is a sense in which an adding machine adds because it represents numbers, but there is a more important sense in which it represents numbers because it adds: We can speak of it as representing numbers only because it stimulates + under some interpretation.

From an explanatory point of view, what interpretation provides is a link between mere state crunching (button-pressing-to-display transitions) and *addition:* Under interpretation, the state transitions of the system are revealed as adding. You can get a feel for the explanatory role of interpretation by imagining that the device is an archaeological discovery. Perhaps you know from documents that the thing is an adding machine; however, looking at it, you have no idea, at first, how to give inputs or read outputs. You can "make it go," let's say, by turning a handle, but this is just more or less random manipulation until you find an interpretation that reveals the state transitions of the device as sum calculations and hence establishes the representational status and contents of those states. To know how to use it is to know how to see it as simulating +, and that means knowing how to "make it go" and how to interpret it.

The concept of representation that is operative here can be brought more clearly into focus by considering again Galileo's ingenious use of geometrical figures to represent mechanical magnitudes (figure 8.1). The crucial point is that, given Galileo's interpretation of the lines and volumes, the laws of Euclidean geometry discipline those representations in a way that mirrors the way the laws of mechanics discipline the represented magnitudes: The geometrical discipline mirrors the natural discipline of the domain. That is, geometrical relationships among the symbols have counterparts in the natural relations among mechanical variables[7] in such a way that computational transformations on the symbols track[8] natural transformations of the system. That is what makes it correct to say that the symbols—lines and volumes—*represent* times, velocities, and distances.

Of course, this is what Galileo *intended* them to represent; that is the interpretation he stipulated. But it is one thing to intend to represent something, another to succeed. Galileo's figures *actually do* represent mechanical variables because the computational discipline *actually does* track the natural one. This is the natural discipline we have in mind when we say that the system behaves according to natural law. I call Galileo's interpretation a proper interpretation because under that interpretation the natural system and the geometrical system that represents it march in step: The geometrical system *simulates* the natural one.[9] A proper

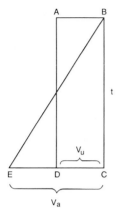

Figure 8.1
Galileo's diagram.

interpretation is an interpretation that gets it right: The symbols actually represent what the interpretation says they represent.

Representation, in this context, is simply a convenient way of talking about an aspect of more or less successful simulation.[10] The volumes behave in the geometrical system in a way analogous to the way certain distances behave in the natural system. Hence, the volumes are said to represent those distances; those distances are proper interpretations of those volumes. For instance, the volume of the triangle tracks the distance traveled by the uniformly accelerated body; the volume of the triangle is the *geometrical analogue* of the distance traveled by the accelerated body. This is what makes it correct to say that the volume of the triangle *represents* the distance traveled by the accelerated body, i.e, that the distance traveled by that body is a proper interpretation of that volume. Representation enters into this story in a way exactly analogous to the way it enters into the story about adding machines. In both cases, it is the fact that one function simulates the other under a fixed interpretation that makes it possible to think of the arguments and values of one function as representing the arguments and values of the other. The causal structure of an adding machine—the fact that it executes an appropriate program and hence satisfies the function *g*—guarantees that the arguments and values of *g* track the numbers; it guarantees, for example, that "3" is the computational analogue (in the machine) of three in the addition function. This is what makes it possible to think of "3" as a symbol *in the system* for three. Analogously, the formal structure of Euclidian geometry guarantees that the volume of the rectangle in Galileo's figure will track the distance traveled by the unaccelerated body, and this is what makes it possible to think of that volume as representing that distance.[11] The analogy between Galileo's geometrical treatment of mechanics and the computational treatment of addition is brought out by noticing that the Tower Bridge picture applies naturally to the former as well as to the latter:

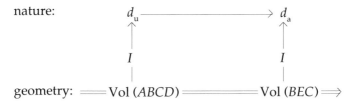

nature:

$d_u \xrightarrow{\hspace{4cm}} d_a$

geometry: $=\!=\!\mathrm{Vol}\,(ABCD)=\!=\!=\!=\!\mathrm{Vol}\,(BEC)\Longrightarrow$

Nature maps the distance traveled by the unaccelerated body onto the distance traveled by the accelerated body; geometry maps the volume of the rectangle onto the volume of the triangle.

s-Representation

The concept of representation invoked by the CTC is the same concept that is implicit in the sort of mathematical science that Galileo invented. It is the sense in which

- a graph or equation represents a set of data
- a linear equation represents the relation between time to solution and the absolute value of the mutiplier when a product is computed by a successive addition algorithm
- a parabola represents the trajectory of a projectile
- intelligence cannot be represented on a ratio scale (when we say "twice as smart," we misrepresent intelligence),

and

- we ask whether social or economic dynamics can be adequately represented by a set of linear equations (knowing that the nonlinear case is computationally intractable).

It will be useful to give this sort of representation a special name. I will call it "s-representation"—"s" for "simulation," because s-representation is simply a consequence of (one might almost say an artifact of) simulation.

Since s-representation is familiar from the context of mathematical modeling, it is useful to list several features of s-representations that are uncontroversial in that context:

- When we are dealing with mathematical models of a natural phenomenon, the criteria of adequate representation are just the criteria of adequate modeling. Typically, we use a battery of statistical techniques to determine how well a mathematical model simulates nature's discipline observed and recorded as "the data." A failure of fit between data and model shows that the model does not adequately s-represent the world (or that aspect of the world that we are trying to s-represent).

- We draw a strong distinction in this context between what we intend to represent, or are trying to represent, and what we succeed in representing. No one would make the mistake of thinking that a linear equation represents the relation between time and distance in free fall simply because that is what someone intended or believed.

- s-representation is also explicitly a matter of degree; the issue is *how* adequate a model is and whether it is better than competitors.

- s-representation is relative to a particular target: A particular linear model may be a better model of system S than it is of system S', but it would be out of place —a misunderstanding—to ask which system, if either, it "really" represents.

- Failures of s-representation are often not "localizable": When a model is not adequate, it is sometimes possible to pin the blame on a particular culprit (the wrong empirical value for a parameter, say), but notoriously, it is often not possible to make more than rather vague and global judgments of culpability.

- There is often a pragmatic element to representation in this context: A linear model of a complex social system may be an adequate representation for some purposes and not others, and may be preferable to nonlinear models simply because it is mathematically more tractable.

All of these points (and, no doubt, more that I haven't thought of) apply to representation in a computational context. When we write programs—even very simple ones—we often *intend* interpretations that turn out to be Improper. The computational discipline we have designed is inadequate, and the desired tracking fails, at least in part. Discussing a bridge-playing program, I might say, to myself or to a colleague, "This data structure represents the opponent's bridge hand." But if the program is a failure, so is the representation. The upper and lower spans of the Tower Bridge fail to connect properly. Strictly speaking, what I should say in such a case is "I meant this data structure to represent (s-represent) the opponent's hand, but it doesn't seem to work."[12] This commonplace experience of programmers highlights the fact that successful representation in computational systems is not simply a matter between the symbol and its interpretation but depends essentially on the processes that have computational access to (are "defined over") the symbol. A bug in the "logic" of a program can lead to a failure of representation—a failure that may well be correctable without altering the data structures in question at all. It follows from this consideration that misrepresentation in programming, like misrepresentation in mathematical modeling, may be a global affair, with no obvious culprit. It is often difficult to say whether unsatisfactory performance is best improved by altering the data structures (i.e., by finding a better knowledge representation), or by altering the processes that operate on them.[13]

As was pointed out above in connection with addition, the fact that s-representation is simply an offspring of more or less successful simulation is often obscured by the common use of "near English" (or some other natural language) in coding data structures in high-level programming languages. If a data structure for a program intended to play bridge has symbols such as "K-clubs," it is natural to suppose that what we have is a representation of the king of clubs. And so we do; that is what "K-clubs" means *to us* in "near English." But "K-clubs" doesn't succeed in representing the king of clubs *in the system* if the program is a radical failure. We must be careful to distinguish what we intend a data structure to represent in the system we are building from what, if anything, it *does* represent in the system, and to distinguish both of these from what it represents in some independent representational scheme such as our own natural language. There is no "further fact" required for successful s-representation beyond what is required for successful simulation.

In programming, as in mathematical modeling, failure comes in degrees; the tracking may be imperfect but not fail utterly. The computational and natural systems mostly march in step, but with lapses in coordination. We can bring out this point, and the analogy with mathematical modeling, by imagining Galileo's system "automated," i.e., realized as a computational system for solving problems of mechanics. As Galileo set up the system, it isn't quite right. Moreover, given the geometry he was working with, there *is* no way to get it exactly right. The Galilean geometry misrepresents mechanical reality; it does not, and cannot, perfectly simulate the natural order. Galileo had an inadequate "knowledge representation," but one that went a long way nonetheless. Thus, in the world of s-representation, misrepresentation differs from failure to represent only in degree; failed representation becomes misrepresentation when the failure isn't too bad. This is especially true if the failures are identifiable and (more or less) correctable or avoidable.[14] We usually think of the case of Galileo as one of misrepresentation rather than one of failure to represent, because his system is a great deal better than the competition was and because we know how to improve performance; that is, we can specify conditions under which the system's performance is quite good—correct "for all practical purposes"—so there is a sense in which we think of it as "being on the right track."

But isn't it more correct to say that Galileo intended to represent mechanical reality but failed? Misrepresentation is representation, after all, not simple failure to represent.

We could say that Galileo failed to represent mechanical reality rather than that he misrepresented it. "Absolutely speaking" (whatever that means, exactly), it is a failure. Relatively speaking—relative to historical context and available competitors—it was a ground-breaking success. Thus, we could say either that Galileo came closer to representing mechanical reality than the competition, or that he represented mechanical reality better than the competition. If we think of matters in the first way, we will not speak of misrepresentation except as a synonym for intended representation that fails to some extent. If we think of matters in the second way, we will say that Galileo misrepresented mechanical reality, but not as badly as, say, Buridan. The important point is that the imagined objection (in quotation marks above) simply presupposes that representation isn't a matter of degree. The underlying thought is something like this: "Either we have representation or we don't have it, and only if we have it can we speak of misrepresentation."

It is all too easy to think of representation as like identification (the speech act), and of the processes that act on them as like predication. Successful identification (hence reference of one kind) is prior to predication, and hence prior to truth. First there is the issue of what, if anything, you have managed to identify; *then* there is the issue of what to predicate of it, and whether the result is something true. But we cannot suppose analogously that first there is the issue of what (if anything) is represented and then there is the issue of what processes act on the representations. What is s-represented is essentially a matter of the processes, for it is essentially a matter of simulation. And simulation is essentially a matter of degree.

s-representation is relative to a target of simulation. Since (as we will see shortly) proper interpretations are not unique, g may be an imperfect simulation of f but a perfect (or better) simulation of g. Indeed, given any f imperfectly simulated by g, it is (I suppose) always possible to find an f' that g simulates better than f. Thus, it makes no sense to speak of s-representation *simpliciter*; s-representation (and, hence mis-s-representation) must be relativized to the function simulated. Given an interpretation function I, g is a more or less accurate simulation of f. Against this background, we can say that some symbol—one of g's arguments or values—accurately tracks (i.e., represents) or imperfectly tracks (misrepresents) its interpretation under I. But the very same symbol may be said to represent or misrepresent something entirely different given a different interpretation under which g simulates (more or less successfully) a different function, f'. Galileo's symbols are imperfect representations of mechanical variables, but they are perfect representations of plane figures in Euclidian space. Geometry is better geometry than mechanics. Big surprise.

Once we admit these relativizations, we can see why nothing comparable to the "disjunction problem" that arises in connection with covariance theories arises for Interpretational Semantics. We needn't *worry* that we can always trade misrepresentation of x for accurate representation of Something Else; we *can* do that, but it doesn't *matter*. The fact that a system satisfying g thereby perfectly simulates f under I has no tendency to show that the system doesn't also thereby imperfectly simulate f' under I'. And it is the fact of simulation (and its degree of adequacy) that bears the explanatory load in the Tower Bridge strategy. No doubt adding machines simulate functions other than +, but that does not compromise the standard explanation of addition in adding machines.

Is this playing fair? Couldn't the covariance theorist pull the same stunt? Here is how it would go: We prefer imperfect correlation with C to perfect correlation with B on the grounds that C, but not B, is an important property of D, where what we are trying to do is explain the system's performance in D (not D', where *B* looms large).

I have some sympathy with this line of defense, but I suspect that this sort of relativization (or lack of uniqueness, if you like) is just what the covariance theorist was trying to avoid. I leave it to the reader to determine whether covariance is worth saving (for some framework other than the CTC) and, if so, whether this move will help.

But notice that Interpretational Semantics allows for cheap representational contents, and learns to live with them by pointing out that their low price doesn't compromise their explanatory role in the CTC. That defense isn't available to the covariance theorist, because covariance theories cannot explain what representation is in a way that is consistent with the CTC.

Interpretation

There is a deep problem about the notion of interpretation that needs to be canvassed before we go any farther. The simple way to understand an interpretation function is to think of it as any one-to-one mapping. But this is evidently much too liberal. To see why, notice that there is a one-to-one mapping between multiplication and addition. Thus, if + interprets g (our button-pressing-to-display function), then so does × (by transitivity of one-to-one mappings). It will follow that g instantiates × as well as +; i.e., anything that is an adding machine is automatically a multiplication machine as well. This is surely unacceptable.

Given this simple-minded and liberal understanding of interpretation, the whole business of getting a system to instantiate a given function f becomes *trivial*. It is not trivial in general; designing calculators was a major achievement, and designing calculators that multiply as well as add was a nontrivial achievement as well. So there must be something wrong with understanding interpretation simply as one-to-one mappings.

Let us return to our example. Let *A* be an adding machine that instantiates $+\langle x, y \rangle = z$ as $g(\langle C, N, +, M, = \rangle) = d$, a function that maps button-pressing sequences onto display states. Now, since the multiplication function, $\times (\langle x, y \rangle) = z$, is one-to-one mappable to

+ , if we take interpretation to be any one-to-one mapping it will follow that A instantiates × as g too. But what is the interpretation function? The obvious choice is this:

$$I_+ (\langle C, N, +, M, =\rangle) = I_\times (\langle C, N, +, M, =\rangle),$$

and if $g (\langle C, N, +, M, =\rangle) = d$, then

$$I_\times (d) = \times (I_\times (\langle C, N, +, M, =\rangle)).$$

There are a number of other possibilities, but—and here are the crucial points—*they all involve computing* ×, *and they all involve ignoring the display*. And that's cheating! It is evidently *cheating* to build the function to be instantiated into the interpretation function, because if you do *that* then you will need *another* system (yourself with paper and pencil, typically) to instantiate the function *directly*, i.e., without cheating. In the example, you will need a multiplication machine to compute the values of $I_\times$. And if you have one of those, why bother with A? It is also cheating to interpret the display in a way that ignores the display. If we try to treat $I_\times$ as a function of the display, we will rapidly get a contradiction. When we enter two plus two, the display will read "4". So $I_\times$ ("4") = 4, since that's 2 × 2. But when we enter one plus three, the display will read "4" again, but we must interpret it as 3, since 1×3=3. $I_\times$ can get around this only by ignoring the display—i.e., by taking the display as a context-sensitive symbol whose interpretation is sensitive *only* to the context.

This particular example can be undercut by requiring that interpretation functions be structure-preserving as well as one-to-one—i.e., by requiring that f and g be isomorphic, which addition and multiplication are not. (In addition, no number plays the role played by zero in multiplication.) But requiring that interpretations establish isomorphism is still much too weak. $x + y$ *is* isomorphic to $2\pi(x + y)$, yet a simple adding machine does not compute $2\pi(x+y)$; it computes $x + y$ and the interpretation has to do the rest (compute $2\pi(z)$).

The obvious moral is that the only really interesting interpretation is what we might call *direct* interpretation. But I must confess that I don't know how to define *directness*. It seems that not building the function to be instantiated into the interpretation function should be a necessary condition, as should not ignoring the arguments and values of the instantiating function. But these are very shaky conditions. First, in any finite device, such as an adding machine, it is possible to get around the first problem—the problem of building the target function into the interpretation—by defining the interpretation function via a (no doubt huge) lookup table. Of course, one would construct such a table by doing the forbidden calculation, but I'm not at all sure how to exploit that fact in formulating a careful definition of what I'm calling *direct* interpretation, because one can obviously *use* such a table without doing the calculations required to build it in the first place. One might counter this move by pointing out, with some justification, that table lookup is a form of computation, and hence that the interpretation does incorporate a computation of the function to be instantiated.

However this may be, some legitimate interpretation surely involves nontrivial calculation, at least for some of us. I am not prepared to disqualify base-3 adding machines just because in order to use them I have to do some translations that, intuitively, are as difficult as adding itself. I suppose someone could get so good at I_x that it would seem like "reading" the product off A's display rather than like calculating it. Something very much like this surely happens when we learn new notations (e.g., Polish notation in logic) or a new language. More important, one doesn't want the notion of interpretation to be tied in this way to what an interpreter has to do; rather, it should be tied to the complexity (or something) of the proposed interpretation function.[15]

The second problem—ignoring the arguments and values of the instantiating function—can be got around by defining an interpretation that is like I_x but does take the display into account in some trivial way. For example, define I_x' as like I_x except that when the display is "5" the interpretation is that there is no answer. This will force an interpreter to look at the display every time to check that it isn't "5".

Reflections such as these make *direct interpretation* seem like a rather subjective and relativistic affair. Nevertheless, it appears to me to be absolutely central to the notion of function instantiation (and hence computation), so I'm simply going to assume it, leaving to someone else the task of filling this hole or widening it enough to sink the ship. *Something* must account for the fact that instantiating f isn't enough to instantiate every function isomorphic to f.[16] I am inclined to accept a kind of transcendental argument for the solvability of the directness problem: The standard Tower Bridge explanation of addition is *correct*, after all, and it presupposes a nontrivial concept of interpretation; therefore, such a concept of interpretation exists. On the strength of this, when I speak of interpretation I will mean *direct interpretation*, assuming there is such a thing. The intuitive content is, after all, fairly clear: Interpretation must be relatively trivial; the system has to do the work, not the interpretation function.

Even on the assumption of direct interpretation, it might seem that if A s-represents anything at all, then A s-represents any content you like. Let g be a button-pressing-to-display function satisfied by S, and let g be interpretable as addition. Let f' be identical to + except that $f'(\langle n, m \rangle)$= Richard Nixon when $n + m =$ 5, and +($\langle n$, Richard Nixon$\rangle$)= +($\langle n, 5 \rangle$). Then g is interpretable as f'—the new intrepretation function is just like the old one except that a display of "5" represents Richard Nixon instead of 5. Thus, we seem to have the consequence that representational contents are not just cheap, they are free. But isn't it clear that calculators represent numbers *all the time*, and that they don't represent numbers most of the time and Richard Nixon on occasion?

The trouble with the argument that saddles us with adding machines s-representing Nixon is that, whereas g simulates f', it isn't really the case that "5" is the computational analogue of Richard Nixon. "5" doesn't track Richard Nixon as he is buffeted about by any natural discipline except the discipline enforced on him by f', which is evidently "cooked up." Once again, I am embarrassed by the fact that I have no general account of what makes f' a degenerate target for simulation, but it seems intuitively clear that f' *isn't* a proper object of simulation, and hence that adding machines don't represent Richard Nixon in virtue of simulating f'.

Whatever one thinks about degenerate simulation targets like the one just described, it is clear that any system that simulates f is bound to simulate a lot of other functions as well—e.g., the numerical function that relates the Gödel number of a standard expression of an argument of f to the Gödel number of a standard expression of f's corresponding value. These won't typically be *familiar* functions, or *interesting* functions, but they will be simulated nonetheless. And this still leaves s-representational content relatively cheap, on the assumption that price varies inversely with supply.[17] We have already seen that the availability of alternative interpretations in no way undermines the explanatory use to which s-representation is put by the CTC. Nevertheless, it is tempting to suppose that some interpretations are improper on grounds external to the facts of simulation—viz., on the grounds that only some simulations matter (i.e., are actually used by a containing system). The idea here is that an s-representation of f isn't a representation of f *to the system itself* unless s-representing f actually has a function in the system. Both Millikan and Dretske utilize this idea, though in different ways. The basic idea is to choose, from among possible interpretations, the interpretation that tracks the function of the process interpreted, and call *that* the representational content. We might call this the selection-by-function approach to representation—a kind of two-phase approach in which we add a functional requirement to s-representation in order to get "the real thing."

The selection-by-function approach can be made very attractive by the following reflection: Whether the inputs and outputs of a program (I include all the data structures a program constructs as among its outputs) should be considered representations at all, or whether (like eggs and hollandaise) they should be construed simply as inputs and outputs, seems to depend on how they are used—i.e., on their *functions*. The inputs and outputs of a recipe *could* be treated as symbols. There is, after all, nothing intrinsic about eggs and hollandaise that unsuits them for a representational career; it is just that no one and no thing actually *does* treat them as representations of something else. And this makes it seem that whether something actually is a representation, as opposed to merely being capable of representing, is a matter of whether it actually gets used as a representation.

The trouble with the selection-by-function approach is that it actually adds nothing new; it enforces no new constraint beyond what is already present in s-representation. What is it, after all, for a computational system to use a simulation of f? Well, the values of f must be arguments for h. Hence, the values of g_f must be arguments for g_h. So what we have here is a super-function F having f and h as components, instantiated as G, having g_f and g_h as components. In short, we have a computation of the values of G. The problem of how the simulation of f is used resolves into the problem of how to interpret the computation of G—i.e., into the problem of what the computation of G simulates. The selection-by-function approach provides no constraints beyond what is provided by the requirement that an interpretation of G must interpret its computation, i.e., its component functions, i.e., the steps of the program execution of which explains satisfaction of G. This is not a trivial constraint by any means, but it will not rule out the alternative numerical (and other) interpretations whose existence is guaranteed by model theory.

Perhaps we could understand use noncomputationally, as Millikan does. But this appears to be no help either. If I and I' are alternative interpretations of a system S having the same domain and isomorphic ranges, then the physical structure that we specify when we say that S has the s-representational content provided by I is the same physical structure that we specify when we say that S has the content provided by I'. For S, having I-content will be nomologically equivalent to having I'-content. Hence, any causal or evolutionary interactions tracked by the fact that S has I-content will be tracked equally by the fact that S has I'-content. The problem is that any causal/selective interactions will be sensitive only to the physical structure, and we pick out by reference to the one content the very same physical structure that we pick out by reference to the other. So it looks as if noncomputational but nonintentional interactions won't distinguish among alternative interpretations. To put the point intuitively, if somewhat misleading: A robot that "thinks" it is simulating a numerical function N will do just as well in E as one that "thinks" it is simulating natural processes in E ', as specified by $f_{E'}$ provided N and f_E are isomorphic. Both will be equally good (or bad) at picking up trash, for example. Narrow content can be a lot narrower than one might have thought!

Cognition

The CTC proposes to understand cognitive systems as systems that computationally instantiate cognitive functions. This idea requires a bit of unpacking.

The CTC embraces a thoroughly rationalist conception of cognition. A system is cognitive, according to this conception, in virtue of respecting epistemological constraints appropriate to its task domain (the domain it is said to cognize). That is, its behavior is cogent, or warranted, or rational relative to its inputs and internal states. This is what makes it correct to think of it as cognizing a domain rather than merely responding to an environment. It follows from this conception that we have no reason to think of a system as cognitive except insofar as we can describe what it does—its capacities—in semantic terms, for epistemological constraints are defined only for propositions, or things with propositional contents—things with truth values, in short.[18] We thus arrive at the idea that having a cognitive capacity is instantiating a function that relates propositional contents, i.e., a function that takes propositional contents as arguments and values and relates them as premises to conclusion. A cognitive system, in short, is an *inference engine*—a system that merits an inferential characterization. Thus, to explain cognition is to explain how a system can merit an inferential characterization— i.e., to explain how it can reason. This is the conception I put forward in Cummins 1983. It is explicit also in Haugeland 1978, Dennett 1978, 1987, and Pollock 1987a. It is at least implicit in the work of those (e.g., Fodor) who think of cognitive systems as systems that realize some form of belief-desire psychology; as

Dennett points out, belief-desire psychology is essentially a psychology of rationality. Under this conception, the problem of cognition becomes the problem of explaining the fact that the system is described by a *cognitive function*, or, for AI, of building a system that is described by a cognitive function.[19]

It is possible to think of cognitive functions as relating intentional states (e.g., beliefs and desires) to one another, since epistemological constraints make sense when applied to these as well. If we go this route, we are free to think of physical systems as actually satisfying (rather than instantiating) cognitive functions. But this wiggle really makes no difference. Cognitive science generally assumes that cognition is a matter of generating the right representations. One then supposes either that the representations have as interpretations intensions (the proposition that Nixon is a crook, say) that are the arguments and values of cognitive functions—in which case we think of those functions as instantiated—or that the representations figure as constituents of intentional states, the intentional states inheriting their intentional properties (being a belief that Nixon is a crook, say) form the semantic properties of the representations (the proposition that Nixon is a crook). Either way, the representations wind up having the same interpretations, and the system winds up instantiating the same abstract function.

The CTC's proposal is that cognitive systems are computational systems: A cognitive system is described by a cognitive function because it computes representations whose contents are the values of the cognitive function, and computes these from representations of the function's arguments. If we suppose that the objects of computation—the things over which the computations are defined—are *symbols*, some of which are *content-equivalent* to the inferential descriptions that figure in the specification of the target cognitive function, we can explain why the system merits inferential characterization, i.e., why it is cognitive: The system merits inferential characterization because it computes symbols representing conclusions from symbols representing the corresponding premises. To move in a disciplined manner from symbol to symbol—to *compute* symbols—is, *under interpre-*

tation, to move in a disciplined manner from content to content. If we get the discipline right, we get inference and hence cognition.[20]

To say that there are cognitive engines, then, is, on this conception, to say that the behavior of certain things is describable via an interpretation that reveals their activity as epistemologically constrained—as rational. Once the rationality of the activity is revealed, we are led to ask how such activity is possible. The strategy employed by the CTC is designed to answer this question by providing a program (computation) and interpretation such that the system executes the program and, under interpretation, execution of the program is revealed as the very cognizing identified as the explanandum. The basic assumption of the CTC is that, under proper interpretation, symbol crunching is cognition.

Semantics enters into the picture because to understand how a physical device could satisfy a cognitive description we need to forge a conceptual connection between computations and inferences (broadly construed). The CTC explains a cognitive capacity by showing how it is computationally instantiated, and this requires linking the arguments and values of cognitive functions. Interpretations specify the links you need to see in order to see computation as cognition (or as addition, for that matter). Objects of computation seen under interpretation—i.e., individuated *semantically*—are representations. We call an object of computation a representation when it is important to see the computation as an instantiation of something else. That is why the display states of a calculator are properly regarded as representations but the outputs of a recipe (as in hollandaise) are not.

It is useful to put the explanatory role of interpretation into a broader perspective. The goal of science is, in part, to develop concepts (or a vocabulary, if you like) that enables us to solve particular explanatory problems. To a first approximation, what a good conceptual scheme does is force us to characterize the system under study in a way that screens out all the information that is irrelevant to the problem at hand, leaving only what is essential. Think of the conceptual scheme provided by Newtonian mechanics as a kind of filter, like a pair of conceptual glasses that allow you to see only what matters for the solution of mechanical problems. Provided with a pair of Newton glasses, when you look at a pool table, what you see is a lot of arrows on a plane normal to gravity. The point at which an arrow originates represents the center of gravity of a ball. The length and direction of the arrow s-represent the momentum of the ball. And it turns out that when you see pool tables that way, you can see them simply as conservers of momentum and kinetic energy. Newton glasses, in short, reveal pool as a certain kind of conservation system. Analogously, the proper semantics—i.e., the right interpretation—will allow you to see certain computations as adding and (if the CTC is right) others as cognizing. A proper interpretation of an adding machine takes a physical process and filters out everything but what matters to seeing addition. The CTC is just the thesis that what works for addition will work for cognition.

The Specification Problem

I will conclude this chapter by briefly sketching a potential difficulty with the CTC. My goal here is not serious criticism. My point is that the criticism in question gives us another perspective on the CTC's explanatory strategy and, hence, on its use of the concept of representation.

Crucial to the CTC's conception of cognitive theory is the idea that there are independently specifiable cognitive functions. The idea is that cognitive capacities can be specified as functions on contents in a way that is independent of the way any particular system instantiates or computes those functions. The analogy with calculating is exact and historically important. Multiplication, addition, sine, square root, etc. can be specified independent of any instantiating device. The function so specified is the upper span of the Tower Bridge. We can then ask whether there is a lower span (a computation) and towers (an interpretation) that will support that upper span. If the same strategy is going to work for cognition, we will need comparable independent specifications of cognitive capacities to form the upper span.[21]

It is becoming increasingly clear that the specification problem is the hardest part of the program. The CTC—which is, necessarily, rationalist to the core—is just the idea that cognizing generally is like doing science: *Automate* Galileo's geometry and what you have, under the appropriate interpretation, is a system that simulates mechanics. But since this amounts to mapping mechanical propositions onto other mechanical propositions that "follow," it is also cognition. Cognition is just computational simulation of "natural functions" via the instantiation of cognitive functions that give a theory of the natural function in question.

But suppose there is no natural function to simulate. Perhaps remembering faces and finding your way home isn't like doing mechanics—can't be like doing mechanics—because these domains, unlike mechanics, aren't governed by laws special to them. The analogy with science makes this seem rather plausible. After all, science works only where there are natural kinds. A science of temperature *per se* is possible only if, as we say, thermal phenomena form an autonomous domain of inquiry. What this means is that thermodynamics is possible only to the extent that thermal phenomena are governed by laws that describe those phenomena "in their own terms"—i.e., autonomously. In contrast, an autonomous special science of clothing is hardly possible, as Fodor (1984a) has emphasized in another connection, because there are no special laws of clothing. Clothing, of course, falls under laws (e.g., the laws of physics, chemistry, and economics), so there is no question that scientific study of clothing is possible. There are also, no doubt, "rules" in the clothing domain: how to dress for different occasions and effects, what needs ironing, what can be washed, and so on. But it is doubtful that these rules could be compiled into an expert system that captures human intelligence in the clothing domain. Perhaps, as Dreyfus and Dreyfus (1985) argue, expert human performance in such domains is, at bottom, not rule-driven but example-driven. But this would mean that we cannot specify the explanandum as a set of cognitive functions that take as arguments and values states of, or propositions about, "the clothing domain." We can have a Rationalist specification of cognition only where we can have a special science. But, while we can perhaps have science anywhere, we surely cannot have a special science for every possible domain of intelligent thought.

It seems to follow that the CTC, like mathematical science, will work only for the cognition of autonomously law-governed domains. The precondition for success is the same in both cases: There must be a well-defined upper span to the Tower Bridge. Special science isn't always possible. If cognition is possible where special science is not—in the cases of clothing and faces of conspecifics, for example—then the CTC's Tower Bridge picture of cognition can't be the whole story.[22]

If, as seems increasingly likely, the specification problem for cognition should prove to be intractable, or to be tractable only in special ways, where will that leave us? I think it will leave us with a kind of biological chauvinism (Block 1978). Cognition will simply be identified ostensively, and hence extrinsically, as *what humans do when they solve problems, find their way home, etc.* We will be left, in short, with Turing's (1950) conception that a cognitive system is just one that is indistinguishable from humans (or other *known cognizers*) in the relevant respects.

Perhaps the CTC could learn to live with this eventuality, but not very comfortably, I suspect. It is difficult to see what methodology will move you from function satisfaction (program execution) to Turing equivalence if the *target*—the human, or whatever—has no known or knowable characteristic function that might be analyzed ultimately into steps that have known computational instantiations. Synthesis works best if the thing you are trying to synthesize has a known analysis. Otherwise, it is trial and error. That is *nature's* way, of course, but it takes a long time. For now, anyway, the CTC has no way to make progress without functionally specifying the target and trying for an analysis that will eventually lead to computational instantiations.

Chapter 9
Functional Roles

Functionalism about Mental Meaning

Functional-role semantics, applied to the problem of mental representation, is just functionalism applied to mental representations rather than to mental states and events generally. Mental states are individuated functionally, according to functionalism. But some mental states—representations, for example—are individuated by their contents. Hence, functionalism implies that mental contents are individuated functionally.

The two most popular flavors of functionalism are computational functionalism and causal functionalism, and this carries over to functional-role theories of mental representation. According to causal versions of the theory, a mental state (or event, or process, or whatever) is a representation, and has the content it has, in virtue of its causal role. Thus, something in the mind is a | cats eat mice |, say, because of the position it occupies in a causal network. We specify the position of a representation in a causal network by specifying the possible causal paths to its occurrence in the system, as well as the possible causal consequences of its occurrence. Computational versions are exactly analogous, with computational role substituted for causal role. Although functional-role theories almost always look to either computational roles or causal roles, it is useful to be able to discuss a generic theory, leaving it open how functional roles are to be understood. It is in this spirit that I use the term "functional role."

"Long-Armed" and "Short-Armed" Roles
Functional-role theories come in single-factor and two-factor forms. The idea behind two-factor versions is that there are two components or aspects to meaning: a functional role, which is entirely "in the head," and an external component, which relates the component in the head to the world (Field 1977, 1978; McGinn 1982; Loar 1982; Block 1986, 1987). Single-factor theories sometimes take functional role to include relations to factors "outside the head" (Harman 1982). For example, a single-factor theory may attempt to incorporate the insights of the so-called causal theory of names by holding that the causal chain that (according to such theories) links the use of a name to an "initial baptism" is part of the functional role of whatever mental representation underlies or is analogous to a name (if any).

Block (1986, 1987) argues that single-factor and two-factor versions are essentially equivalent on the ground that two-factor theories simply divide functional roles into two components: an internal or "short-armed" component and an external component which, when added to the "short-armed" component, makes a single "long-armed" component and hence a single factor.[1] The point of distinguishing an internal and an external factor is just to capture the notorious distinction between wide and narrow content (Putnam 1975; Burge 1979, 1986). All two-factor theories assume that it is possible to factor things into internal and external components—an assumption made plausible by the following reflection: We want to develop a theory of cognition that allows for the possibility of the same cognitive system's encountering radically different environments. The possibility of a two-factor approach follows from this desideratum and from the assumption that the desired theory will still be a content-based theory. The content that is alleged to remain constant across changes in environment is narrow content.

Computational and Causal Roles
It is seldom noticed that causal roles are bound to differ from computational roles. This follows immediately from the fact that different causal architectures can instantiate the same computational architecture. But it follows also from the more mundane

point that a given computational state of a system is bound to stand in a mass of causal relations that have nothing to do with its computational status. Only the causal arrows that eventually link the state to other computational states matter.[2] This may, of course, implicate states and processes that themselves have no computational interpretations. But many causal relatives will be left out—e.g., those that are too small, or too distant in space or time, to effect the outcome of the computation. The difference will be especially pronounced if we assume that functional roles are long-armed, for, although there are surely some computational roles that don't stop at the skin, the external causes and effects of representational states will surely have the external computational causes and effects as a small subset. One might try to make the two equivalent by restricting attention to the causes and effects a state has *as a representational state*—i.e., to the causes and effects that a state has in virtue of its representational status and content. But this will not do; the functional-role theorist is trying to define representational status and content in terms of functional roles, so it would be circular to *identify* the relevant functional roles by reference to a state's representational status and content.

Since there are bound to be causal differences where there are no computational differences, but not vice versa, it follows that a causal-role theory allows for distinctions of content that are not allowed by a computational-role theory. This might be thought to show that causal-role theories are inconsistent with the CTC on the ground that the CTC assumes that cognition, and hence content, supervenes on computation. But the CTC needn't assume that every distinction of content derives from a distinction in computational role; it need only assume that distinctions of content not mirrored by computational differences make no difference to cognitive capacities (i.e., to target explananda). An advocate of the CTC is free to accept a causal-role theory provided he or she also holds that, as a matter of fact, distinctions of content relevant to cognition will turn out to be "narrower" (i.e., less finely distinguished) than content in all its causally determined subtlety. It is not legitimate to complain against this that differences in content not reflected in computational role entail differences in cognition not reflected in computational role and hence entail that the CTC is false. The trouble with this complaint is that it simply *assumes* that every difference in content must make a cognitive difference.

The argument for this assumption is typically that my Twin Earth duplicate or Burgean counterpart will have different beliefs and desires than I, yet these differences will not be reflected in different computational roles. This is true. But it doesn't follow that I and my Twin Earth duplicate or Burgean counterpart have different cognitive capacities in the sense of "cognitive capacity" in which the CTC seeks to explain such things. Just as content may be wide or narrow, so may cognition. The CTC evidently seeks to explain cognitive capacities narrowly construed, i.e., construed as the sort of ahistorical capacities that a system might bring to bear on radically different environments, and that might be realized in radically different stuff.[3]

Functional Roles and Conceptual Roles

Though they are often not distinguished in the literature, what I am calling functional roles must be distinguished from what are commonly called conceptual roles. As the name implies, conceptual-role semantics, applied to mental representations, is the idea that a mental state is a representation, and has the particular content it does, in virtue of the role it plays in cognitive processes such as inference. According to this theory, one can locate a mental representation—a |cat|, say—in a cognitive network by considering the possible *cognitive* consequences of occurrences of a |cat| in the system and the possible *cognitive* paths to occurrences of a |cat| in the system.

Conceptual-role semantics, then, is the doctrine that something is a representation, and has the content it does, in virtue of its cognitive role. It follows that conceptual-role semanticists make no provision for representation in noncognitive systems. They thus imply (suggest?) that the representation of numbers in a cognitive system is a fundamentally different affair than the representation of numbers in calculators.[4] Tying representation essentially to cognition in this way seems perverse from the viewpoint of the CTC, which, as we saw, takes cognitive representation to be of a piece with representation in computational systems generally: It is an absolutely central thesis of the CTC that representation in cognitive systems is exactly the same thing as representation in computational systems generally. This is why computation and representation can be thought of as independently available to *explain* cognition. The CTC's proposal is that cognition is just very sexy computation and representation—phenomena that are uncontroversial and relatively well understood in the context of many noncognitive phenomena. This proposal loses most of its bite if we think of representation as a kind of by-product of cognition. It is rather natural to think of representation in this way if you begin by thinking of representation in terms of belief and desire—i.e., in terms of the propositional attitudes; for then representational systems are the things with beliefs and desires, and these are, as Dennett and many others have pointed out, essentially cognitive systems: Belief-desire explanations make sense only in a context in which cogency conditions are respected. The upshot is that we get representation and content tied essentially to rationality, as in Dennett. In chapter 10 I will argue that it is a mistake to think of representation as a kind of corollary of the presence of beliefs and desires. For now, it is enough to notice that the CTC certainly does not so conceive it: Calculators represent but are not belief-desire systems.

Another thing to notice about conceptual-role semantics is that it provides for narrower contents than functional-role semantics. Functional roles—i.e., causal or computational roles—will allow for distinctions of content not allowed by conceptual roles, since there are bound to be computational and causal links not mirrored by cognitive links. For example, almost all computational processes have "side effects" that are (or should be) irrelevant to the logic of the program. Are we to simply assume that genuine cognitive systems are free from "side effects?"[5] More subtly, part of the computational role of | cat | might include the computational consequences of storing it "at the wrong address," or those of buggy access.[6]

Why allow for distinctions in content that are not reflected in any difference in cognitive role? The answer, of course, is that cognitively equivalent states may yet have different contents (Putnam 1975; Burge 1979). If we can argue that computational or causal factors not mirrored in cognitive role sometimes determine content, then an advocate of the CTC who holds a conception of cognitive capacities that provides for sameness of capacity across different computational or causal realizations will want to distinguish a narrow aspect of content that exhibits the same constancies. But the CTC certainly does not dictate such a move. The CTC must hold that the capacities it seeks to explicate retain their identity across differences in *noncomputational factors*. It must therefore cleave to the viability of a kind or aspect of content that is narrow with respect to causal and historical factors not mirrored in computational architecture. But computationalists are free to choose whether to allow for contents distinguished on computational but noncognitive grounds.

Again, one must be careful with "noncognitive." One must resist the move to *define* cognitive differences in terms of content differences, thus making cognitively equivalent states with different contents a contradiction in terms. From the perspective of the CTC, the distinction is unproblematic; the thing to keep your eye on is that there can be computational processes that are insensitive to differences in meaning that are determined by factors irrelevant to the success or failure of simulation. The computationalist is free to concede that these are differences in content, but not in the kind or aspect of content that matters to the specification or explanation of the capacities targeted by the theory (*viz.*, capacities that remain constant across different environments and histories).

There is a temptation to think that conceptual-role semantics is not even a candidate for a *naturalistic* account of mental representation, since it helps itself to the concept of a cognitive process. Students standardly make this complaint. One then smiles knowingly and *explains*. The standard functionalist strategy, in this case, is to define all cognitive processes and states together in terms of the abstract structure of nonsemantic and nonintentional relations (e.g., causal or computational relations) that these processes and states have to one another and to inputs and outputs (see Block 1978). Thus, *ontologically,* the suggestion is the same as in the case of functional-role theories (and interpretational semantics, for that matter): To harbor a representation is to harbor something with the right computational or causal role.

But I think the standard student complaint is on to something. The canonical second-order reduction gives us an ontologically naturalistic specification of what it is to be, e.g., a | cat |, but it doesn't provide us with a solution to the problem of representation as we have been conceiving that problem. Conceptual-role theory tells us in what structure of natural relations a state must be imbedded to have a content, thus satisfying the requirements of ontological naturalism. But it doesn't tell us anything about why the natural structure picked out is the right structure beyond telling us this: It is the structure that, in some particular physical system, happens to realize that system's cognitive structure. Thus, when we ask what it is about some particular node in the structure that makes it a | cat |, the only possible answer is this: It is that thing that stands in the computational/causal relations that realize the inferential and other cognitive relations characteristic of | cat |s. And this means that the theory can't give a noncircular answer to the central question about representation.

I do not mean to suggest that the theory can't define what it is to be a | cat | in purely nonintentional, noncognitive terms; it can. The point is, rather, that the theory gives us no clue as to what it is about the abstract structure it picks out, and what it is about some particular node in that structure, that makes *that* structure a cognitive structure, and *that* node a | cat |. It just gives us an ontologically naturalistic identification of the | cat |s without giving us a solution to the problem of representation. It leaves us wondering why occupying a particular position in a network of abstract relations should amount to *having a meaning.*

Notice how all this differs from interpretational semantics. There, we begin with some function *f* to simulate. Assume that cats appear as arguments or values of *f*. If *S* satisfies *g*, and *g* simulates *f* under interpretation *I*, then the element of *g* (hence state of S) that I maps onto cats is a |cat| in S. The crucial points are these:

(i) f's being a *cognitive* function is irrelevant to whether something in the system is a |cat|. The interpretational semanticist doesn't tie representation to cognition, and therefore allows for the central insight of the CTC that representation in cognitive computational systems is the same as representation in computational systems generally.

(ii) Interpretational semantics brings out the central fact that it is a state's role in a *simulation* that makes it a representation, and the fact that what makes it a |cat| is that its role in that simulation is to track cats.

Ontologically, conceptual-role semantics and interpretational semantics are equivalent. If a certain abstract cognitive structure C is realized in a computational architecture A, then A will simulate C, and hence A will have C as a proper interpretation, with the item realizing the |cat| role interpreted as a representation of cats. And if A simulates a cognitive structure C, then it certainly "realizes" C in the sense required by the standard second-order reduction. But interpretational semantics provides an explication of the concept of representation (s-representation) and its explanatory role in the CTC that is present in the conceptual role-approach only in a question-begging form.

This equivalence between interpretational and conceptual-role approaches holds whether we take conceptual roles to be long-armed or short-armed, and this has an interesting consequence. If, following Harman, we think of conceptual roles as "long-armed"—i.e., as stretching out into the world, and into the past (and the future?)—then we are also thinking of cognitive architecture and its instantiating architecture as "long-armed." To some this may seem good news, for to see matters in this way is to see cognition as instantiated by a system that includes the environment of the organism. On the other hand, it should give pause to those who looked to organism-environment interactions to make contents unique in a way that they admittedly cannot be if we restrict ourselves to "what is in the head," for cognitive interpretations of organism-plus-environment systems will be no more unique than cognitive interpretations of "what is in the head." The added complexity, of course, will make viable interpretations that much harder to come by, but there will still be countably many if there are any. It follows from the equivalence between interpretational semantics and conceptual-role semantics that long-armed conceptual roles provide no stronger constraints on representational content than interpretability.

That including the environment doesn't give us interpretational uniqueness should come as no surprise. The idea that relying on connections to the environment could uniquely fix mental content evidently presupposes that there is a unique best way to specify those environmental factors. But what will this be? Since we are specifying roles, our specifications had better be psychologically projectable (because we want regular counterfactual supporting connections with mental states) and physically, chemically, biologically, economically, . . . projectable (because we want—or anyway, are stuck by the theory with— regular counterfactual supporting connections with other environmental events). The idea of "long-armed" functional roles thus presupposes a homogeneously specifiable causal or computational network that covers both organism and environment. Of course there are such networks (the one given by thermodynamics, for example), but the idea that there is a sort of unique causal network here, with the organism being simply a proper part, is simply outlandish. The most plausible candidates— mechanics and thermodynamics—will not serve up the right contents for things like | cat |s and | shirt |s. (See Fodor 1984b.)

The point I made against conceptual-role approaches—that they provide no explication of the concept of representation or of its explanatory role in the CTC—can be made against functional-role approaches: They provide us with no hint as to why being a node in a network of computational or causal relations should make something a representation or endow it with a particular content. Moreover, it must be confessed that what I have been calling functional-role theories are really straw men; no one actually holds them. A functional-role theorist has no motivation for picking some causal or computational architecture and electing it to the office of representation embedder. The whole idea makes sense only if we suppose that we have some antecedently specified function the realization of which will be a representational system. This, of course, is how interpretational semantics sees matters. From this perspective, the functional-role approach just *is* interpretational semantics with about half the story missing. It is like conceptual-role semantics in not providing an explication of the concept of representation, but it is like interpretational semantics in not tying representation essentially to cognition.

Conclusion

The conceptual-role or functional-role approach to representation is a natural by-product of a familiar "quick and dirty" argument for functionalism about mental content. One begins with an ontological question: What is it in a person's head—my head, say—in virtue of which my states are contentful? On what does content supervene? The answer provided by the CTC is relatively straightforward: I am a thinking system in virtue of the computational structure of my brain. Thoughts, and contentful states generally, must be what they are in virtue of their place in that structure. But a thought is what it is in virtue of its content. So having a content—e.g., being a I the cat is on the mat I —must be a matter of occupying the right role in a computational structure! Right?

The trouble with this way of proceeding is that one *begins* with a human being—something assumed to be a thinking system from the start—and *then* asks simply how content must be realized in humans. This opens the way to saying that it is the computational structure of the human brain, whatever that turns out to be, that must do the job. One skips right over the question of what sort of functional structure will realize contentful states, and why. It's just whatever functional structure humans turn out to have, this being guaranteed to be the right sort of structure (given computationalism) by the fact that humans are known to be cognitive/representational systems.

But functionalism as a theory of mental representation gives us no clue as to why having a computational role should make something a representation or give it a particular content. Indeed, it obscures why computational theories of cognition should traffic in semantics at all. The functional-role formulation provides no hint as to how computationalists should answer Stich's (1983) Challenge: Given that the causal and the computational impact of a data structure are tracked by its nonsemantic properties, their semantic properties need not (and hence should not) enter into any causal or computational explanations that feature them. So why treat them as representations at all?

Functionalism, by identifying mental states with their roles in the production of behavior, suggests that the explanatory project of the CTC is to explain behavior—indeed, to explain stimulus-to-response connections (now called I/O behavior)—at a level of abstraction that isn't neuro-chauvinist by tracking the causal routes through the system via the abstract computational properties of its states. Functionalism thus encourages us to think of mental states as causal mediators, and hence as things whose explanatory role is to make possible a story about the causation of behavior. When a functionalist comes to think of representation, therefore, it is inevitable that the problem should be posed thus: What is the role of representation in the causal mediation of behavior? Once we combine this picture with computationalism, it is hard to see how the concept of representation could do any serious work, and we wind up with Stich's syntactic theory of the mind. Functionalism, since it misrepresents the explanatory role of representation in the CTC, leaves us with Leibniz's worry (see *Monadology*, p. 17). It leads us to ask "What makes a mere syntactic engine a semantic engine?"—a question bound to make us wonder, with Leibniz, how meaning gets into or attached to the cogs and wheels. And once we have come this far, the honest answer is the one Stich gives: Meaning doesn't do any work, so forget it.

Standard over-the counter functionalism therefore leads us to misconceive the use to which the concept of representation is put by the CTC. For the CTC, representation is simply an aspect of simulation. In the special case of cognitive functions, this takes on a special significance for philosophy, though it is nothing special to the CTC, because when the simulated function is cognitive, meaning maps a mechanical process onto a rational one, revealing mind where there was only mechanism. But the concept of meaning has a life in the CTC only as the child of interpretation. Meanings *just are* what interpretations provide. Interpretation is the fundamental notion here; *meaning* is just a name for the product. And to understand the notion of interpretation in the context of the CTC you must understand its explanatory role, which is to map a computational process onto another process, revealing the former as an instantiation or a simulation of the latter.[7]

Chapter 10

Interpretation and the Reality of Content

In this chapter I will discuss three objections to interpretational semantics as an account of the nature of cognitive representation in the CTC. There are two sorts of objections one might make. One might object that interpretational semantics is bad Philosophy of Science; that it does not correctly represent the nature of content as that notion is used by the CTC. I shall have nothing further to say about that here. But one might also object to interpretational semantics in a way that reflects on the CTC itself: If interpretational semantics is an unacceptable account of mental semantics, then perhaps the CTC should be abandoned on the ground that it is built on unsound foundations.

I have some sympathy with this second line of attack. Interpretational semantics, it seems to me, provides the only viable account of representation as that concept is used in the CTC (similarity, adaptational role, and covariance all being incompatible with the CTC, and there being no other candidates in the offing). But, while it is consistent with the CTC, perhaps interpretational semantics isn't really very plausible in its own right. And perhaps its weaknesses point to fundamental weaknesses in the CTC. One such weakness has already been suggested: If there is no well-defined cognitive function to instantiate, then there is nothing to be made of the idea that some element of an instantiating function satisfied by a cognitive system is the computational analogue of an element of the instantiated function, and hence nothing to be made of representation. Representation has no clear sense for the CTC when the domain to be simulated isn't autonomously law-governed. The CTC seems unable to account for cognition of such domains (if there is any).

Objections Introduced

The first two objections to be considered here have to do with the idea that interpretational semantics compromises the "reality" of content in some way, and the third has to do with the relation of representation to intentionality. I shall introduce these objections briefly and then discuss each in detail.

Naturalism   To some, it seems that interpretational semantics rules out a thoroughly "naturalistic" account of content, i.e., an account of content that does not presuppose semantic or intentional notions. This charge, if sustained, would not, by itself, show that interpretational semantics is not realistic about content. Nevertheless, to those inclined to accept some form of physicalism, an account of cognitive content that does not make it amenable to "naturalistic explication" in this sense will be unacceptable; from a physicalist point of view, failure to assimilate cognitive content to the natural order is tantamount to undermining its reality. Compare Fodor:

> The worry about representation is above all that the semantic (and/or the intentional) will prove permanently recalcitrant to integration in the natural order; for example, that the semantic/intentional properties of things will fail to supervene upon their physical properties. What is required to relieve the worry is therefore, at a minimum, the framing of *naturalistic* conditions for representation. That is, what we want at a minimum is something of the form '*R represents S' is true iff C* where the vocabulary in which condition C is couched contains neither intentional terms nor semantical expressions. (1984b, p. 232)

The causal status of content   Another worry, closely related to the worry about naturalism, has to do with the causal status of content. Consider this remark by Dretske:

> Something possessing content, or having meaning, may *be* a cause without its possessing that content, or having that meaning, being relevant to its causal power. Shrieking

obscenities may shatter glass but the semantics of these acoustic vibrations (their meaning) is irrelevant to their having this effect. . . . Following Davidson, we can say that reasons are causes, but the problem is to understand how their *being* reasons, how their *having* semantic content, contributes to their causal efficacy. (1985, p. 32)

The worry here is a species of the one about naturalism: It might seem that if we account for content in a way that blocks its assimilation into the *causal* order, then our theory of content leaves it without genuine scientific work to do, and hence without the scientific reality that it evidently is assumed to have in cognitive science.

Intentionality   A different kind of worry about interpretational semantics has it that the theory allows the CTC to forge no link between representation and intentionality (i.e., between s-representation and the ordinary attitudes) because representational content as construed by interpretational semantics is radically nonunique and relative in a way that the contents of our cognitive states are not. There is thus a serious question as to whether it will be possible to formulate a satisfactory account of the content of beliefs and desires that is consistent with the CTC construed as interpretational semantics construes it.

Naturalism

Does interpretational semantics offer an account of the semantic properties of cognitive systems that does not presuppose intentional or semantic notions? Does the interpretationist satisfy the "naturalistic constraint" expressed by Fodor in the quotation above?

It might seem that the essential reference to interpretation in the interpretationist account is bound to lead to a violation of the restriction against semantic/intentional notions in explicating the semantic properties of cognitive systems. The interpretationist suggestion is this:

(IS) R represents x in S iff there are functions g, f, and interpretation I such that S satisfies g, g simulates f under I, and $I(R) = x$.

It should be clear from this formulation that IS invokes no "interpreter" (an intentional/cognitive agent that does the interpreting), only an interpretation function. The existential quantifier has the sense it generally does in mathematics: The existence of interpretation in this sense doesn't imply that anyone or anything has actually interpreted R.[1] Of course, any actual application of the Tower Bridge strategy to S will involve constructing an actual interpretation. But when theorists assign an interpretation to R, they do not thereby *endow* R with semantic properties; they merely state a hypothesis that might or might not be true, *viz.*, that S actually does simulate f under that interpretation.

We should be careful not to overemphasize this point about naturalism, however. Conceptual-role semantics is, as we saw, ontologically naturalistic but ideologically barren when it comes to explaining representation. What our discussion of conceptual-role semantics should teach us is that an ontologically naturalistic "definition" of representation may be of very little philosophical or scientific interest. Still, there is some independent interest in noting that interpretational semantics is "naturalistic" in the sense recommended by Fodor.[2]

The Causal Status of the Contents of s-Representation

A much more interesting version of the worry about naturalism has to do with the causal status of content as that notion is understood by interpretational semantics. Consider the remark by Dretske quoted above. That quotation comes from a paper in which Dretske's topic is the role of content in ordinary propositional-attitude explanation (folk-psychological explanation, as it has come to be called). The worry that motivates Dretske, however, is a species of a more general worry: If contents are not *bona fide* members of the causal order, then they are *epiphenom-*

ena—nothing happens because of content *per se*. And if nothing happens because of content *per se*, then appeals to content have no genuine explanatory role to play in serious science.

Almost everyone is prepared to allow a causal role *of sorts* to content. A fairly widespread view seems to be that the states of a system that have content have causal powers, and that appeal to these causal powers is, or might be, central to psychological explanation. But it is generally held that the states in question have their causal powers not in virtue of having the contents they do, but in virtue of something else, e.g., their electrochemical potentials or their activation levels and connections.

Dretske is quite right in holding that this view—the Received View, I'll call it[3]—makes content causally inert. But does it follow from the causal inertness of content that it can have no serious explanatory role? This further conclusion seems to require identifying serious explanation with causal explanation—an identification we should resist quite generally, whether the subject is chemistry, physics, psychology, or history.[4] It seems, then, that there are two aspects to the question before us: What sort of causal role (if any) is played by content (as construed by interpretational semantics) in the CTC? Is the explanatory role of content in the CTC a causal role, i.e., is it part of the Tower Bridge strategy to appeal to contents as causes? I'll consider these in order.

Content and Causation

There are, I think, two claims we can focus on when we wonder whether content is a cause:

> (S)   There are true singular content-ascribing causal state-ments in which a cause (or causal factor) is identified via its content.[5]

> (G)   In a true singular content-ascribing causal statement, having the content ascribed is (at least sometimes) the "causally relevant factor."

As Dretske points out, it is the latter claim, G, that is of real interest. Everyone seems to accept S, but the Received View denies G.

Let us begin with an example. Since the CTC is inspired by reflecting on computers, we will do well to take an example from that domain. Suppose that, in the course of executing my word-processing program, my computer executes the instruction JP Z 3b24 (read: If the contents of the accumulator equal zero, load the contents of the address 3b24 into the program counter). And suppose that the address 3b24 contains the instruction INC A (read: Add one to the contents of the accumulator). finally, suppose that the contents of the accumulator equal zero when the first instruction is executed. Then

> (E1)   The accumulator's having the content *zero* caused it to have the content *one*.

Is this content causation? It is certainly enough to verify S, but what about G? Is it the content that is the "causally relevant factor," or is it rather the electronic properties of the states to which contents are assigned, as the Received View would have it?

I think there are only two ways to think about G: the Way of Generalization, and the Way of Counterfactuals.

The Way of Generalization   One reason for rejecting G—the reason that typically underlies the Received View, I think—is that when we come to generalize singular content-ascribing causal statements, we find that the lines of nonaccidental generalization are traced out, not by content, but by such things as electronic properties or patterns of activation or abstract shape. We don't find, the objection goes, that all x's with content C are (whatever), but rather that all x's with a certain electronic property or activation pattern or abstract shape are (whatever). One might hold, as it generally has been held, that the best evidence one could have that F is a causal factor in a singular causal connection is that the corresponding generalization (over F) is observed to hold and is not equivalent to some generalization not referring to F, and that the best evidence for rejecting F as a causal factor is that the corresponding generalizations are not forthcoming. The Way of Generalization bids us to accept G if singular content-ascribing causal statements generalize along lines traced by content, and to reject it otherwise. The Received View is that we should reject it. Consider our example. Of course, it is not true, in general, that the accumulator's having the content *zero* causes it to have the content *one*, but it is pretty easy to fill things out to get the relevant generalization:

> (E2)   Whenever the accumulator represents *zero* and the program counter represents an address containing an instruction to increment the accumulator, the accumulator (subsequently) represents *one*.

E2 is, as we say, "hardware independent." All it requires are (i) some things that function as addresses, the states of which are capable of representing instructions; (ii) something that functions as an accumulator, the states of which are capable of representing zero and one; and (iii) something that functions as a program counter, the states of which are capable of representing addresses. This generality can be achieved only by specifying states in terms of their representational contents and, correlatively, specifying functional units in terms of their representational capacities. On the other hand, the corresponding generalization concerning the electronic properties is going to be limited to Z80's.

If we follow the Way of Generalization, then, we will oppose the Received View and accept G on the strength of examples like the one just rehearsed. Moreover, the argument need not, and typically does not, depend on computer-based examples. There is a familiar abstract argument for accepting G. The argument has two parts: (1) A cognitive capacity is specified, according to the CTC, by a cognitive function, i.e., by a system of generalizations that are or approximate epistemic rules. Since epistemic rules are generalizations defined over things with truth values, it follows, as we noted in chapter 8, that the generalizations in virtue of which something counts as cognitive, are going to characterize that thing in terms of content. Thus, if there are cognitive systems as envisaged by the CTC, there are generalizations involving content ascriptions. Moreover, (2) these generalizations involve content ascriptions essentially; they are not going to reduce to (be replaceable by) non-content-ascribing generalizations because things with different electronic properties or abstract shapes or patterns of activation can satisfy the same content-ascribing generalizations. If one follows the Way of Generalization, G follows from (1) and (2) and the existence of cognitive systems as envisaged by the CTC. The CTC is committed to the causal efficacy of content if we assess causal efficacy by following the Way of Generalization. Of course, (1) doesn't give us *causal* generalizations in the sense in which this literally means a generalization of a singular causal statement that generalizes the causal claim itself. E2 isn't a causal generalization in this literal sense either. (I suppose the literal causal generalization corresponding to E2 is something like this: Whenever the program counter represents an address containing an instruction to increment the accumulator and the accumulator represents *zero*, cycling the system causes the accumulator to represent *one*.) Asking whether we are justified in generalizing the causal claim itself, however, buys us nothing; the only grounds we could have for generalizing the causal claim itself would be the truth of instances in which content is the causally relevant factor, and that just brings us back to G.

As it was formulated above, the argument that semantic properties make generalizations possible focuses exclusively on the instantiation of cognitive capacities. This is the way the argument is usually stated (e.g., in Pylyshyn 1984). But, as we have seen, the CTC regards representation as a feature of noncognitive computational systems as well. Thus, the argument could just as well be stated in terms of the broader class of computational systems that instantiate or simulate other functions. Systems that instantiate the same function—all adding machines, for example— have something in common that can be captured by only generalizing over semantic properties (as I just did). There is nothing special about cognitive functions in this connection, and hence the causal status of content rests on no special thesis about cognition held by the CTC.

The Way of Counterfactuals   Another approach to evaluating G is to ask whether singular content-ascribing causal statements support content-ascribing counterfactuals. From our example, we have the following:

> (E3)   Had the accumulator not represented *zero* at *t* it would not have represented *one* at *t'*

However, we also have this:

> (E4)   Had the accumulator not had EP-O at *t* it would not have had EP-1 at *t'*. (Think of EP-O as an electrical engineer's specification of whatever electronic property the accumulator has when it represents a one, and similarly for EP-1.)

Both E3 and E4 are pretty clearly true. Moreover, there is a suspicion that E3 is only a reflection of E4 in just the way it would need to be to undermine G in favor of the Received View. What we need, it seems, is a counterfactual that does not have a true analogue formulated in terms of the underlying electronic properties.

Is there such a thing? The prospects seem dim. As long as we stick to counterfactuals that, as it were, stay securely pointed at a particular incident—at a particular change and its cause—we are bound to find what we found with E3 and E4. Counterfactuals of that kind are not sensitive to the way in which the events are picked out; they are *de re* in this respect, and hence they provide no leverage to distinguish between E3 and E4.

To get around this problem, we would have to consider counterfactuals that relate *types*—an incrementing of the accumulator or the like. But evidence for counterfactuals of that sort is just going to be evidence relating *types*, i.e., evidence for generalizations. Thus, if we take this route, we gain access to no source of evidence bearing on G beyond what we get by following the Way of Generalization.

It seems, them, that we are left, unsurprisingly, with what any scientist would have said: G rests on the possibility of confirming content-ascribing generalizations. Since such generalizations are presupposed by the CTC, advocates of that theory are bound to accept G as well and accord to content whatever "reality" or membership in the "natural order" goes with having a causal role.[6]

This should come as no surprise. The CTC's central strategy is to get the formal structures—the representations—to march in step with the things represented. If the symbols track the meanings, the meanings are bound to track the symbols. But the symbols track the meanings because of the causal structure of the device, so the meanings are bound to track the causal relations among the symbols. That contents can be used to track the causal transactions of a system will follow trivially from the assumption that the system instantiates a function having those contents as arguments and values.

Still, the feeling remains that it is the syntax (or the electronics) that does the causing, not the content. In the Tower Bridge picture, it is the bottom span that represents causation in the system, not the upper span; the upper span just *mirrors* the lower one. Knock off the upper span and the lower one would go on just as before. Isn't that how it seems?

This is a misunderstanding. You can't "knock off" the upper span. Its presence is *entailed* by the structure realized in the lower span: If g instantiates f in S, then $g(x) = y$ entails that $f(I(x)) = I(y)$. Once you have built the lower span, you have built the contents; there is nothing more to s-representation than instantiation. The very fact that entitles you to say that $I(x)$ is a content of x will guarantee that the g-transformations of x—lower-span causation—are tracked by the f-transformations of $I(x)$. To the extent that this fails, representation fails as well, and you do not have a content to start with. S-representational descriptions of S are available only to the extent that the interpretations line up with arguments and values of functions satisfied by S, so s-representational descriptions are going to be exactly as causal as descriptions in terms of functions satisfied.

Content Causation and Explanation by Content
Taken together, (1) and (2) constitute an argument for what might be called an autonomous semantic level of analysis for cognitive systems (Pylyshyn 1984): The CTC assumes that cognitive sys-

tems can be described by a set of content-ascribing generalizations that are autonomous in that they don't reduce to non-
content-ascribing generalizations. Moreover, the CTC is, as we
have just seen, in a position to avail itself of the usual reasons for
supposing that states of cognitive systems have effects in virtue
of their contents. But nothing we have said implies that the
explanatory role of content in the CTC has anything to do with its
causal status or with the fact that there are important and autonomous content-ascribing generalizations. And in point of fact, the
Tower Bridge strategy assigns no explanatory role to these generalizations; it identifies them as the *explananda* of cognitive science. The discovery of such generalizations is, of course, crucial
to cognitive science as the CTC sees it, for to discover such
generalizations is to specify the cognitive capacities of the systems under study.[7] But to identify the explanatory role of content
in the CTC with the subsumption of particular events under
content-ascribing generalizations would be a double mistake: It
would misrepresent what it is about cognitive systems that the
CTC wants to explain, and it would totally miss the most distinctive feature of explanation-by-content in the CTC (namely, that
under interpretation a mere computational process—and ultimately a merely physical one—is revealed as a simulation or an
instantiation of another process). Interpretation systematically
interrelates analyses on two different dimensions[8] hence, when
we see a process in terms of its interpretation—i.e., in terms of its
s-representational contents—we see it as something else. The
turnings of cog wheels, for example, are seen as steps in a division
algorithm.

Intentionality

Representation, as interpretational semantics understands it, is a
very simple affair: S s-represents the arguments and values of
any function it simulates. As we saw in chapter 8, it doesn't
follow from this that S represents anything you like. It does
follow, however, that representational contents are radically
nonunique. Representational contents, we discovered, are deliv-
ered relatively cheaply by interpretational semantics. But, al-

though the CTC can live with the idea that adding machines simulate other functions besides +, it seems quite impossible for the CTC to live with the idea that when I think about Central America I am also inevitably thinking about a number. There are surely countless numerical propositions that have never been, and never will be, the content of any of my thoughts. And yet my data structures (assuming, with the CTC, that I have them) surely represent numbers if they represent anything, since anything with any systematic interpretation is bound to have a systematic numerical interpretation. How are we to reconcile the nonuniqueness of representational content with the obvious fact that my thoughts about Central America are not about numbers?

S-representation and intentionality   As I am using the term here, a system with intentionality is a system with beliefs, desires, and (perhaps) the other ordinary "folk-psychological" states individuated by content. Thus, to have a belief with the content that U.S. policy in Central America is dangerous is to be in an intentional state, as is seeking the fountain of youth. Simply to harbor a data structure with the content that U.S. policy in Central America is dangerous is not, so far, to be in an intentional state. We must be careful to distinguish mere s-representation, which is cheap, from intentionality, which is expensive. The contents of thoughts—typical adult human thoughts, anyway—are quite amazingly unique and determinate. When I think the thought that current U.S. policy in Central America is ill-advised, the proposition that current U.S. policy in Central America is ill-advised is the *intentional content* (not to be confused with the intended content) of my thought. The proposition that current U.S. policy in South Africa is ill-advised is not the intentional content of that thought (though it may be something I believe, and hence, the intentional content of a different one of my thoughts). It is commonplace to hold that the intentional content of a thought can be the proposition p but not p' even though p and p' are logically equivalent. (See Stalnaker 1984 for a dissenting view.) And if George Bealer (1984) is right, it is possible to have a thought that is about a rabbit without thereby having a thought that is about an instance of Rabbithood.

Thus, although there is some dispute about the exact price, there is no doubt that intentional contents are expensive. But so what? Why should the fact that intentionality is so *nice*, so *discriminating*, be an embarrassment to those who hold that representation in the CTC is not? Sheer confusion is sometimes at fault, I suppose. Representation and intentionality are not always distinguished. But the real issue goes much deeper. The real issue goes back to what I called, in chapter 2, the representational theory of intentionality (RTI).

According to the RTI, intentional states inherit their intentional properties from the semantic properties of their constituent representation. My thought is about Central America not about a number (the Gödel number of "Central America", say) because the data structure on my BELIEF BLACKBOARD represents Central America and not a number. It is obvious that this theory will never do if one accepts interpretational semantics, for interpretational semantics entails that the data structure on my BELIEF BLACKBOARD *does* represent a number (though we may not know how to express the numerical function that is instantiated).

Nor can we bring intentional content into line with representational content by relativizing the former in the way we relativized the latter. It just isn't true the former in the way we relativized the latter. It just isn't true that my thoughts about Central America are about Central American only relative to some choice of domain (function to be simulated) and interpretation. A data structure s-represents different things under different interpretations, but thoughts don't represent in that sense at all. They are just about what they are about. Interpretational semantics must reject the RTI. Thus, if I'm right about the CTC's being committed to interpretational semantics, the CTC must follow suit and reject the RTI as well.

This incompatibility between the CTC and the RTI helps to explain why the problem of representation has seemed so difficult. The RTI is rather popular among those sympathetic to the CTC. The RTI requires that representation be *discriminating:* Since I can think about mice without thereby thinking about shrews, even though I can't tell the difference, the RTI will require that I be able to represent the one without thereby representing the other.[9] This is the problem to which Lockean covariance theories and Millikan's adaptational-role theory address themselves. Perhaps, under ideal conditions, a |mouse| would show up in my percepts just in case I were confronted by a mouse; a shrew wouldn't cause a |mouse| under ideal conditions. Or perhaps the mechanism that "interprets" (responds to) a |mouse| in me has been replicated in me because of historical transactions with mice, not with shrews. If you assume the RTI, or anything else that lines up representational contents with intentional contents, the problem of representation will look very much like the problem of intentionality; the central issue will be to devise an account of representational content that individuates them as finely and as uniquely as intentional contents are individuated—i.e., as finely and as uniquely as beliefs are individuated. If, however, you are not attracted to the RTI or to anything comparable, then you are free to strongly distinguish the problem of intentional content from the problem of representational content, and hence free to adopt an account of representation that makes representational content cheap. You are free, in short, to accept the CTC and the interpretational semantics that goes with it. Or so it seems.

Can the CTC ignore intentionality?   It is tempting to suppose that no theory of cognition can afford to ignore intentionality, since cognition is essentially an intentional phenomenon. If you think of cognizing as a matter of getting into intentional states—as belief fixation, say—then the CTC hasn't a chance of explaining cognition, for to explain how I managed to get into the right intentional state is surely in part to explain how I got into a state with the right content (*viz.*, the content of that intentional state). What the CTC *can* do is explain how you got into an s-representational state having that same content. But that won't be nearly enough, as we have seen. Getting into an s-representational state will not explain why the intentional state has the content it has *and no other*, since the s-representational state in question is bound to have other contents. Thus, it is certainly true that, if cognitive functions are intentionally specified, the CTC must explain intentionally specified functions, and this will require more than mere s-representation.

But, of course, this doesn't settle the matter. It is not at all obvious that cognitive functions must be, or even *can* be, intentionally specified. The CTC, as I have had occasion to emphasize before, seeks an *individualistic* psychology, i.e., a psychology that focuses on cognitive capacities of the kind that might be brought to bear on radically different environments.[10] If the anti-individualistic position with regard to intentionality is right (i.e., if beliefs and desires cannot be specified in a way that is independent of environment), then the explananda of an individualistic psychology cannot be specified intentionally. It follows that the CTC shouldn't—indeed *mustn't*—concern itself with intentionally specified explananda. What the anti-individualist arguments of Putnam and Burge prove from the viewpoint of the CTC is that beliefs and desires aren't psychological states in the sense of "psychological state" of interest to the CTC.

But are there individualistically specifiable explananda for a theory like the CTC to target? Certainly. Notice, first, that the CTC is not limited to the explanation of cognitive functions. The Tower Bridge strategy has a wide range of applications outside of cognition in which representation plays the same role that it plays in the CTC's alleged explanations of cognitive functions. This is worth emphasizing because we need to keep in mind that the CTC, unlike typical philosophy of mind, begins not with beliefs and desires but with the computational simulation of variously specified functions. The proposal about cognition is simply an extension of this strategy. The extention is to be effected by considering functions that embody epistemological constraints appropriate to some task. Functions respecting cogency conditions need not, in general, be specified in intentional terms (i.e., in terms of belief and desire), though they do need to be specified in semantic terms. The function specifying deductive validity is an obvious case in point. To refuse to call cogency-respecting operations cognitive simply because their arguments and values aren't beliefs or other intentional states is surely to quibble about words.

Advocates of the CTC, then, needn't worry that the narrowness or the nonuniqueness of s-representational content relative to intentional content will deprive the CTC of legitimate employment in cognitive science. But the CTC owes us *some* account of intentionality. Or, rather, it must be possible to give an account that is consistent with the CTC if the CTC is to be viable. And if not the RTI, then what?

Adding intentionality to the Tower Bridge   The inevitable suggestion at this point is that we combine a causal or adaptational account of intentionality with the CTC, so that s-representation plus some further constraint external to the CTC (e.g., causal or adaptational or social context) equals intentionality:

$$s\text{-}representational\ content + FC = intentional\ content.$$

One possibility is to think of FC as a kind of filter that selects the intentional content of a data structure from among its s-representational contents. If we keep in mind the fact that the explananda of the CTC are not intentionally specified and hence are not specified in terms sensitive to FC, it is evident that the CTC puts no substantive restrictions on the choice of FC.

Twin Earth cases (Putnam 1975) have, I think, made this "filter" strategy seem plausible to many. Imagine a system S that simulates a bunch of H_2O functions (functions having H_2O as argument or value). S-twin, its twin on Twin Earth, will simulate only XYZ functions isomorphic to S's H_2O functions (otherwise they won't be twins). It follows that any simulation of S's H_2O functions will be a simulation of S-twin's XYZ functions. Hence, S will simulate S-twin's XYZ functions and hence s-represent XYZ exactly as well as S-twin. But—and here is the Putnam punch line—S, unlike S-twin, bears FC relations to H_2O but not to XYZ, so S's beliefs are about H_2O and not about XYZ. S *Intends* H_2O but not XYZ, whereas S-twin *Intends* XYZ but not H_2O.

This strategy is a representationalist theory of intentionality in that, like the RTI, it implies that each intentional content attributable to S is a content of some representation of S's. The content of each belief, for example, is held to be a privileged s-representational content of some data structure—namely, the one that satisfies FC (the "further constraint"). On this view, the RTI is half right: Intentional states are still relations to internal representations. However, what determines the intentional content of a representational state goes beyond what determines the content of that state required by the CTC for its proprietary purposes. The CTC needs only s-representational content; but representationalists about intentionality are free, in pursuit of their own explanatory goals, to select intentional contents from among the s-representational contents of CTC's data structures. The data structure underlying a belief, on this view, isn't a belief, nor is any computational relation to that data structure a belief. It is, rather, a BELIEF—a sort of CTC-supported narrow-content counterpart of a real belief, *viz.*, something that is a belief when we enforce FC. This makes the difference between BELIEF and belief look like a philosopher's nicety that cognitive scientists pursuing the CTC can afford to ignore; it makes it look as if advocates of the CTC can go right ahead and talk just like "folk psychologists" so long as they keep the caps lock down.

Tempting as this is, we should proceed with caution. There is, after all, no *a priori* reason to suppose that there are such things as BELIEFS and DESIRES. The proponents of the CTC should consider the possibility that the narrow psychological component of a particular belief, say, is not a "local" state of the system but a "global" one. Even if we are entitled to the assumption that belief factors into an s-representational component and some other component harnessed by FC, there is so far no reason to assume further that the narrow psychological component—the CTC-supported component—is a BELIEF, i.e., a characteristic functional state of the system with an s-representational component whose semantic properties, together with the "further constraint," account for the intentional properties of the BELIEF. Perhaps the truth is, rather, that (to borrow a metaphor from Quine 1960) a belief stands in relation to the CTC-supported psychology as the overall shape of a hedge stands in relation to the intricate pattern of individual twigs and leaves. Or, slightly less metaphorically, a belief stands in relation to the CTC-supported psychology as a "point of view" stands in relation to an editorial: There may be no particular bit of the editorial that expresses the point of view; the whole editorial does it. Moreover, countless other editorials, different in detail and even in subject matter, might express the same point of view. So, perhaps, your entire psychological state underlies each of your beliefs and desires, and underlies them in such a way that a quite different psychological state might ground the very same beliefs and desires.

If this view of the matter (let's call it *globalism*) is correct, then there are no BELIEFS and DESIRES, and the RTI isn't even half right. Just as no one sentence need express the point of view of an editorial, so there need be no particular representation underlying any given belief. Perhaps it remains true that one has the beliefs one has in part because of the information represented in one's head, but it will not be true that the content of a belief will be even loosely traceable to some particular representation. From a globalist perspective, FC is a function from global computational state to belief (or whatever), not from BELIEF to belief.

Globalism is attractive for a number of reasons:

- There aren't enough data structures to go around. Representationalism about intentionality requires a data structure for every belief, and there seem to be more beliefs than data structures. (See, e.g., Dennett 1978.) The standard reply is that some beliefs are *derivative* in that we have them only in the sense that they are derivable from beliefs that correspond to actual BELIEFS. But I know of no empirical evidence for this view that isn't better evidence for globalism.

- There are, according to the CTC, lots of data structures that are nonstarters as BELIEFS —for example, the $2\frac{1}{2}$ - dimensional sketches invoked by computational theories of vision, or the phonological representations invoked by speech-recognition theories. Perhaps these are to be disqualified by function: They don't display the right computational role to be BELIEFS. Or perhaps, if we just knew what FC was, we would see that it doesn't apply to cases like this. Whatever the distinction might be, it is hard to see how it could have a principled motivation in terms of concepts internal to the CTC.

- Globalism is attractive because it provides a natural explanation of the well-known mushiness and relativity of belief attribution (Dennett 1987; Stich 1983). If globalists are right, attributing a belief is going to be a little like attributing a point of view to an editorial. Some cases are going to be uncontroversial, but many will leave room for rational observers to disagree, to be uncertain, and to fall back on pragmatic considerations and rough estimates. Since that is the way belief attribution *is*, and globalism would explain that fact, perhaps globalism is true.

- Finally, globalism is attractive *to me* because it removes any temptation to assimilate the problem of representation to the problem of intentionality. As globalists (if not convinced, at lease open-minded), we will not simply *assume* that THE PROBLEM for advocates of the CTC is to somehow attach intentional contents to data structures.

Final reminder: How not to play the representation game   It is easy for philosophers of mind to start thinking about representation by getting involved in the following pattern of thought (with variations of order and dependency): Talk about cognition is talk about what is rationally assessable—i.e., about the stuff to which epistemology applies—and that includes beliefs (primarily) and perhaps desires and actions. Now, the CTC, it is rumored, says that representation has to do with cognition, and this we philosophers can applaud as quite correct; beliefs, after all, are individuated, and (more important) are epistemologically assessable, in virtue of their contents. Thus, the problem of mental representation that the CTC raises is just the problem of intentionality, i.e., the problem of getting the contents of beliefs attached to the representations supplied by the CTC.

This rather common philosophical outlook on the problem of representation is a mistake in (at least) three ways.

- It assumes without argument that something like theRTI is true—i.e., that having beliefs involves harboring representations whose contents are equivalent to those beliefs. But the full RTI is incompatible with the CTC, and the CTC by itself provides no reason to endorse any form of representationalism about intentionality.

- It assumes that the explanatory role of content in empirical theories of cognition (such as the CTC) is just the explanatory role of content in belief-desire psychology, though perhaps "cleaned up" a bit for the lab. And this couldn't be further from the truth.

- It ties the notion of representation essentially to cognition (intentionally specified cognition, in fact), thereby blocking our vision of what is most distinctive about the CTC's approach to cognition—namely, its claim that representation has the same role in explaining cognition that it has in explaining the capacities of computational systems generally.

The cure for all this is to approach the problem of representation as a philosopher of science rather than as a philosopher of mind. First determine what explanatory role representation plays in some particular representation-invoking scientific theory or theoretical framework; then ask what representation has to be—how it should be explicated—if it is to play that role.

It is, of course, perfectly legitimate to wonder about intentionality—to wonder, for example, what determines intentional contents, or what distinguishes one kind of intentional state (e.g., belief) from another (e.g., desire). And it is legitimate to wonder how intentionality relates to representation. But it is not legitimate to invent representation to order, or to present the representation-invoking sciences with an ultimatum to provide philosophy with the missing piece to its puzzle about intentionality or get out of Mindville.

Chapter 11

Connectionism and s-Representation[1]

A connectionist architecture consists of a network of connected nodes. At a given moment, a node is characterized by a variable representing its level of activation and by a constant representing its threshold. When the activation of a node exceeds its threshold, activation is propagated from that node to others along whatever links happen to exist. Links are weighted, the weights determining the (relative) quantity of activation they may carry. Connection weights may be positive or negative: that is, a given node can *inhibit* the nodes to which it is connected by a negatively weighted arc by subtracting from their activation. The state of the network at a time is given by the pattern of activation at that time (i.e., the activation level of each node at that time) and by the connection strengths.

An input is given to the network by providing some specified level of activation to nodes designated as input nodes. Activation then spreads throughout the network in a way determined by the antecedently existing pattern of activation and by the strengths of connecting links. The *dynamics* of the system is given by differential equations that determine activation spread as function of time. The "output" of the system is the state of that portion of the network designated as the output nodes when the entire network "settles down" into a steady state. As a result of certain "back-propagation" processes,[2] the connection strengths may be altered, thereby altering the input/output function the network satisfies. This is how such systems "learn."

Interpretation

On the standard view of matters, if connectionist networks are to be cognitive engines, they must be capable of satisfying cognitive generalizations. Since these are stated in semantic terms, networks must have semantic interpretations.[3] There are two ways of semantically interpreting connectionist networks. *Localist* approaches assign interpretations to individual nodes. For example, in the well-known word-recognition model of Rumelhart and McClelland (1982), a node can represent such things as the presence of a certain feature (e.g., a horizontal line intersecting a vertical one), the presence of a particular letter (e.g., "A" or "L" or "H"), or the presence of a given word (e.g., "READ"). A localist network is interpreted as a whole by noting which nodes are activated; the interpretation of the network is simply the composition of the node interpretations.

Distributed approaches to representation assign interpretations only to network *states*. Since a given network state *s* can be thought of as a superposition of several states, it is possible to think of *s* as the composition of the interpretations assigned to the superimposed states. In distributed approaches, individual nodes need have no representational function.[4]

The Conservative Connectionist

The computational theory proposes to explain cognition on the assumption that cognitive functions are computationally instantiated. The idea is that the objects of computation—the things over which the computations are defined—are *symbols*, some of which s-represent the arguments and values of the cognitive function targeted for explanation. For example, the system merits inferential characterization because it computes symbols that represent conclusions from symbols that represent the corresponding premises. To move in a disciplined manner from symbol to symbol—to *compute* symbols—is, *under interpretation*, to move in a disciplined manner from content to content. If we get the discipline right, we get inference, and hence (one kind of) cognition.

The picture that goes with this strategy is just the Tower Bridge picture introduced above in chapter 8:

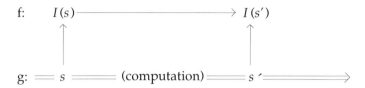

The central ideas behind the CTC's approach to cognition are the following:

> (i) The objects of formal computation are symbols whose contents are the arguments and values of cognitive functions.[5]

> (ii) A system has cognitive capacities in virtue of its capacity to compute the cognitive functions specifying those capacities.

We get the right value from a given argument because the causal structure of the system implements a program that links symbols whose interpretations are the appropriate arguments and values of the cognitive function to be explained.

At this *very* abstract level, what we might call "conservative connectionism" can be seen to embrace the same explanatory strategy as the CTC: A cognitive capacity is explained by showing that the arguments and values of the corresponding cognitive function form a proper interpretation of the arguments and values of a function satisfied by a physical system. From this very lofty perspective, while all of the interesting substantive detail is lost to view, a certain similarity of conception emerges: Conservative connectionists can be seen to share a conception of content with computationalists insofar as they share a conception of content's explanatory role, viz., a conception of content as an interdimensional mapping from the subsemantic to the explicitly cognitive. For the conservative connectionist, representation is s-representation, as it is for the advocate of the CTC, for representation plays the same explanatory role in both cases: It links the upper span of the Tower Bridge to the lower span.

Prospects for a Radical Connectionism
Is connectionism, then, simply another instance of the Tower Bridge strategy?[6] It needn't be. To represent a radical alternative to the CTC's explanatory strategy, however, connectionism must deny either idea i (above) or idea ii. I will consider each of these options briefly before proceeding to a more detailed discussion.

Option A   What happens to the connectionist picture of things when we insist on a distinction between the objects of computation and the objects of interpretation? Well, on this view of things, representations aren't computed.   Connectionists pay a large price for this option, for it amounts to denying any direct explanatory relevance to computation.   Option A retains the orthodox idea that we have disciplined relations between contents *because* we have a disciplined relation between symbols having these contents, but denies that computation imposes the relevant discipline on the symbols! If this isn't the *Mystery Theory of Cognition*, it will do until the real thing comes along.[7] All the processing goes on "below" the symbols, as Smolensky's (1988) word "sub-symbolic" rightly suggests, leaving the symbols free of any visible discipline. (Nice for them, but bad for explanation.) The bottom span of the Tower Bridge is not connected to the superstructure:

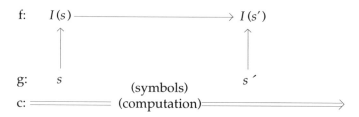

Option B   Radical connectionists who are allergic to Mystery may wish to retain idea i—the idea that representations are computed—and argue instead that their approach differs from that of the CTC in denying the existence of the upper span in the Tower Bridge picture.   They needn't abandon s-representation *entirely;*

they will still want to hold that individual nodes instantiate numerical functions, for example. But they must abandon the idea that there is any representation of the arguments and values of cognitive functions. But then what? If connectionist systems are to be cognitive systems, they must, it seems, simulate cognitive functions somehow. And surely that just *entails* that states of the system are *representations* interpretable as the arguments and values of cognitive functions. Option B doesn't appear to be coherent.

What is the radical connectionist to say—*Mystery* (option A), or *Incoherence* (option B)?

Creative Salvage

Perhaps things are not as hopeless as they appear on the surface. Let us examine the options a bit more sympathetically and creatively.

Option A   The central idea is that the relevant symbols aren't computed. Instead, they *emerge* (evolve?) as artifacts of computations over something else (*viz.*, activation levels and connection strengths [8]) in something like the way in which the temperature of a gas "emerges" as the result of molecular interactions that are themselves described in thermally neutral terms. Something like this is, I think, the received view among thoughtful connectionists (see, e.g., Smolensky 1988). The difficult thing to do is specify the relation between the computations and the supervening symbols in a way that makes the supervenience *principled* but doesn't lead back to the conclusion that the symbols are objects of computation after all (albeit computation on a more abstract level than that featuring individual nodes and connections). It is not enough to point out that connectionist computation can be described at the level of nodes and connections, a level at which the objects of computation have no cognitive significance. After all, the fact that we *can*, in principle, describe orthodox computation at the bit (hence numerical) level has no tendency to show that orthodox systems don't compute symbols whose contents are the arguments and values of cognitive functions. As I was at pains

to emphasize above, it is precisely the fact that CTC programs have a description at the level of cognitively significant symbols that grounds the orthodox explanatory strategy in its application to cognition.

The difficulty with denying i can be brought out clearly by considering the two ways in which connectionist networks are interpreted. If the interpretation is local, we evidently have a system in which the objects of computation are identical with the objects of interpretation, since it is activation levels of individual notes that are computed, and that is precisely what the localist interprets. To deny idea i, then, the radical connectionist must insist on distributed representation.

Assume, then, that the objects of interpretation are activation levels of arrays of nodes. On this view, activation vectors are the symbols whose contents are the arguments and values of cognitive functions, but it is the activation levels of individual nodes that are computed. Hence, the objects of computation are distinct from the objects of interpretation.

But this distinction is an illusion. Given an algorithm for computing the activation levels of individual nodes, it is mathematically trivial to construct an algorithm for computing the activation vector whose elements are computed by the original algorithm. It is, of course, a mere change in notation.[9] We are thus still faced with the problem of how to deny idea i while not endorsing the Mystery Theory of symbol discipline.

The only suggestion I have ever heard is that, although the algorithm defined over the distributed representations is possible, it is not the right algorithm to look at for explanatory purposes. The idea is familiar in a way: It is possible, as noted above, to describe an orthodox AI program at the bit level, but that is the wrong level for explanatory purposes. So perhaps it is possible to argue that a connectionist algorithm defined at the level of activation vectors (distributed representations) is the wrong level of explanatory purposes. But this idea appears difficult to sustain in the face of the obvious fact that separating the objects of computation from the objects of interpretation creates an explanatory gap rather than closing one, for it leaves unexplained why the symbols are appropriately disciplined.

Option B   If connectionism is to retain the idea of symbol computation, there must be some principled way to connect the computation—the bottom layer of the picture above—to the symbols. This is evidently impossible if the symbols are not to be arguments and values of any function the system actually satisfies. So we must, after all, connect the bottom level of the picture with the symbols:

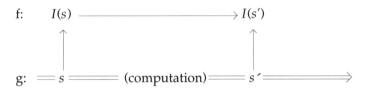

This, of course, is just the old orthodox picture. Just looking at the picture, you can see that there is only one way to break the rectangle that defines the orthodox picture while retaining the idea that the system computes symbols: Erase the line between the interpretations!

The result is a system that computes symbols but that doesn't s-represent anything; the significance of erasing the top line is that there is no function *f* to simulate; no natural discipline in which the interpretations of the symbols are embedded and that is mirrored by the computational discipline of the system. Thus we have a picture that requires a notion of representation quite different than that required by the CTC: covariance, perhaps, or adaptational role.

The notion of representation isn't the only thing that is different. The picture above leaves us with no *explanandum*! How are we to understand what our radical Type B connectionist is up to?

As it happens, I have already sketched an answer. At the end of chapter 8 I worried aloud that there may be no cognitive functions as conceived by the CTC, or precious few, and speculated about how the problem of cognition would have to be reconceived if the "specification problem" were to prove intractable. On the option currently being considered, we will continue to conceive of cognitive behavior as essentially meaningful behavior. That is, we will continue to think of cognition in a way that makes it appropriate to think of a cognitive system as a system that moves in a disciplined way from representation to representation. However, what makes such behavior cognitive will be understood not in terms of any discipline embedding whatever is represented (we have removed that from the picture) but *comparatively*, as Turing (1950) understood it.

Turing defined an intelligent system as one that is indistinguishable from a normal adult human *as a question answerer*, or, more generally, *as a communicator*. Cognitive behavior thus conceived is still behavior under an interpretation, and hence behavior naturally explained in terms of the computation of representations. But it is not behavior conceived as the simulation of an intrinsically specifiable cognitive function, and hence it is not behavior that must be thought of as explained by a program—a computation—embodying a *theory* of question answering. And this, perhaps, is where the true brilliance of the proposal lies, for no such theory may be possible.

What the Type B radical connectionist needs to do, then, is develop a generalization of Turing's conception of cognition (or intelligence, if that is more appropriate in this scheme of things)—a conception that does not limit cognitive behavior to linguistic behavior of some kind, but retains the idea that cognitive behavior is essentially behavior under a semantic interpretation. The last clause is essential, for (to repeat) only behavior that is conceived as behavior under interpretation (like Aristotle's *actions*, as opposed to his *motions*) is naturally explained by appeal to the computation of representations.

Option C   Once we deny the existence of cognitive functions—once we deny that the point of interpretation is to construct a link between a computational capacity and an independently disciplined relation on propositions—a large part of the motive for semantic interpretation is removed (though not all of it, as we have just seen in discussing option B). Some will be tempted, having come this far, to simply abandon representation altogether, i.e., to abandon the idea that the states of the system are fruitfully individuated by semantic properties.

The idea being suggested here—abandoning representation—should not be confused with Dennett's (1978) idea that cognitive contents are not represented but, as I put it elsewhere (Cummins 1986), *inexplicit*. This is really an impossible idea to pursue in a connectionist context, because the distinction between what is explicitly represented and what is merely implicit (e.g., in the state of control) is a distinction that makes sense only in an orthodox programming context. Explicit contents are contents of data structures; everything else is implicit. Connectionists must reject the data structure/process distinction that generates the explicit/implicit distinction in the CTC. A connectionist system that merits cognitive characterization because it simulates cognitive functions will fall under the Tower Bridge picture. If there are states of the system that have arguments and values of cognitive functions as interpretations, that simply makes the interpreted states s-representations. Perhaps they aren't data structures, but all that means is that they are not the objects of "read" and "write" operations. We still have cognitively relevant s-representations that are the objects of connectionist computation, and that just leads us back to the orthodox Tower Bridge Picture.

What I have in mind for option C, then, is the radical idea that semantic interpretation plays no role whatever in the connectionist scheme of things. The result is option B taken a step further. The requirement that cognitive behavior be conceived as behavior under an interpretation is dropped, and hence the implication (retained in option B) that cognitive behavior is to be explained as the computation of representations is dropped. Cognitive performance, on this conception, becomes purely ostensive and comparative: To the extent that a system performs comparably to a normal adult human doing distinctively normal adult human tasks, that system is "intelligent," or "cognitive." There is just nothing else to be said. It is behaviorism of the old school, with the following slight revision: Neurophysiology, which is where behaviorists thought talk of internal states belonged, is replaced by something slightly more abstract—a mathematical model of neural dynamics. The result is pretty much what radical behaviorism envisaged all along: We have psychology discovering "effects"—i.e., non-semantically characterized regularities in human and animal performance—and a nonpsychological explanation of the underlying mechanism. Not quite neuroscience, on this variation, but close.

I would be dishonest if I didn't close by saying that I hope this kind of empiricism about cognition—the kind of computationalist behaviorism just described as option C—proves unnecessary. For if this is the way we go, ultimately, then in a deep sense we will have to admit that cognition can't be understood, at least not in its own terms. There will be scientific study of cognition, as there can be scientific study of clothing, but there will be no science of cognition *per se*. Such an approach might even allow us to duplicate cognition artificially, but cognition would resist autonomous scientific characterization.

What I really hope is that the conservative connectionist will turn out to be on the right track. One exciting possibility is that connectionist systems can be used to *solve* the specification problems that bedevil the orthodox in the current state of things. For connectionist systems can be taught (often by psychologically unrealistic feedback, but never mind) to do things that CTC systems have to be programmed to do. To program a system to simulate a cognitive function, you have to have a specification of the target function. You have to have a serious analysis, in fact. But to teach a connectionist system to simulate a cognitive function, all you need to know is what the right output should be on any given cycle. This suggests the following methodology: Train the thing up until it does pretty well by Turing-type standards, then (and here is the piece that is missing so far) recover the wanted analysis from the system.

Why suppose that this will work? Well, it may be that we (WE) have trouble with the specification problem because the relevant concepts are missing. We, as scientists, think like consciously reasoning linguistic agents. And this, as has often been pointed out, limits our horizons. The things that give orthodox AI trouble are things that we do so automatically that we don't know how we do them. We have no set of concepts for describing how we do such things; and we are not likely to develop them in the normal course of affairs, because the processes they apply to are literally beneath our notice. Brains, of course, figure it out, or have it innately. But brains are difficult to analyze, physically or mathematically. An artificial computational system, on the other hand, can be so analyzed. So perhaps that is where the payoff might lie: a system that doesn't need to be programmed to perform, but which is easier to analyze than a brain.

Notes

Chapter 1

1. I owe this way of putting the contrast to Georg Schwarz (1987).
2. Locke, the first explicit causal theorist I know about, arrived at covariance by a different but related route.
3. You get this sort of theory by taking Dretske's (1986) idea that x represents y if it is x's function to covary with (indicate) y and combining it with the common idea that functions should be understood in terms of evolutionary history (c-ing is x's function if x's c-ing is what accounts for the fact that xs get replicated.) Millikan, of course, didn't arrive at the theory in this way.
4. A theory that distributes meanings over symbols *in the general case* (i.e., without relativizing to language or speaker, etc.) would, it seems, have to be a theory of meaning proper.
5. Beliefs are said to be about things, but not to refer. And we don't speak of the meaning of a belief, or what a belief means, except in the sense of natural meaning: Jon's belief in Creationism might mean that he is a fundamentalist Christian.
6. Connectionist theories are certainly computational theories in some sense, but they differ from the theories I have in mind in that representations in connectionist models are not symbolic data structures over which the primitive computational operations of the system are defined. To repeat a point made earlier: Connectionists do not assume that the objects of computation are the objects of semantic interpretation.
7. The general practice in philosophy these days is to use "mental representation" or "cognitive representation" as a generic term for any state of a cognitive system that is individuated by semantic content. This simply blurs the distinction between representational states (e.g., data structures) and intentional states (e.g., beliefs).
8. Fodor calls this theory the representational theory of mind. This name is quite natural if you tend to think of mentality as what I am calling intentionality: If psychology (cognitive psychology, anyway) is exhausted by a theory featuring the propositional attitudes, then the representational theory of intentionality *is* properly called the representational theory of mind.
9. This section draws heavily from Cummins 1986, a paper that should have been called "Inexplicit Content."

10. "Inexplicit representation" is, I take it, a contradiction in terms. For some content to be explicit in a system is just for it to be the content of some representation—i.e., (in the CTC) the content of some data structure. In orthodox computational systems, whatever isn't the content of some data structure isn't explicit.

11. It seems likely that consciousness is nomologically necessary for the sort of biologically based thought that we are familiar with on Earth. But that could well be an accident of evolution.

Chapter 2

1. Those who assume that intentional states such as belief and intention are possible only in virtue of the capacity for representations and their manipulations—e.g., those who assume the RTI—will be launched on a regress. In order to explain the beliefs and intentions of the subpersonal agencies, they will have to suppose that, in addition to the mental representations that those agencies use to communicate with one another, there are other representations, internal to each agency, that ground the intentional states of that agency. How are they to account for the semantic properties of *these* representations? Perhaps it it worth pointing out that this regress is distinct from the regress of intentions sometimes thought to bedevil Gricean accounts of meaning because the communicating agent's intention must itself be intended to have a certain effect. That regress doesn't arise, however, if the intentions in question can be self-referential. (See, e.g., Searle 1983.)

2. Homuncular formulations of functionalism encourage the idea that some form of intended-use theory could work for mental representations because, although the posited homunculi are less sophisticated than a full person or cognitive system, they are still conceived as intentional agents. See section iii.7 of Cummins 1983 for a discussion of the confusion between intentionality and intelligence.

3. For an attempt to work out a neo-Gricean theory in an AI context, see Cummins 1982.

4. See Putnam 1975 and Burge 1979, 1986. See Loar 1985 for a mildly dissenting view.

Chapter 3

1. The following brief discussion owes a great deal to Haugeland (1985).

2. The area of the triangle, of course, is half the base times the height: $(v/2) \times t$. To see that this is the distance traveled by the accelerated object requires some mathematical reasoning that was not formulated explicitly until the invention of the integral calculus, 33 years after Galileo's death!

3. I am inclined to see this idea—the idea that nature can be grasped and understood by finding ways to map the world onto symbols in such way that mathematics disciplines the symbols as nature disciplines the things symbolized—as *the* idea in the birth of modern science.

4. Well, of course, cats and cartoons cats are both material objects; indeed, they

are both *organic*, what with newspaper's being made of wood pulp and all. More important, there is similarity of color. But there is no similarity of shape or weight or biological properties—the sorts of properties that distinguish cats from dogs, say, or similarly colored cats from each other. There is no hope of making anything out of the real similarities.

5. I suppose Berkeley should, in a sense, be credited with discovering this problem, for (famously) Berkeley held that ideas could not represent mind-independent things (for example, their causes, whether material or divine) on the grounds that an idea cannot resemble anything but another idea. However, rather than draw the obvious conclusion that representation doesn't depend on similarity, Berkeley concluded only ideas could be represented by ideas. Given a choice between two solutions, philosophers generally pick the more perverse one.

6. This discussion owes a great deal to J. Bennett (1971).

7. It is easy to get confused about this. The point is not that it makes sense to ask of any physical thing with a shape "is it hexagonal or isn't it?" but rather that, if the thing has a shape at all, it has some particular shape — the shape it has—whether or not that shape has a name. A sample triangle made of plastic cannot "agree in shape" to both oblique and scalenon triangles.

If you put together three rigid telescoping rods with hinges at the ends, you can fit this to any triangle that isn't too big or too small. But now you have cheated, because what matters now is not (or not only) the similarity but the procedure itself. See the discussion of color matching below.

8. Not only is the similarity between chip and target now inessential, it just gets in the way. Suppose you have a device like a light meter—a color meter. You point it at a colored object, and it gives you a digital display: RED (or whatever). With this, you could determine that the chip and the target are similar in color. But why bother? Forget the chip; point the color meter at the target!

Chapter 4

1. The resemblance theory has a similar problem: Not all resemblance counts as representation. And the cure is pretty much the same: *x* is a representation in virtue of its function (*x* is an *idea*, say), and *x*'s specific content is fixed by resemblance.

2. This model is not, of course, meant to be taken seriously. The idea is to have a sample architecture as a context in which the covariationist approach to representation can be illustrated.

3. In fairness, it should be pointed out that Locke hoped to extend the doctrine as described above by exploiting a distinction between simple and complex ideas. Thus, it seems clear that Locke thought we could have a concept of *elementary particle* by having the concept of *particle* and the concept of *divisibility*. This evidently requires some recursive apparatus that gives us the content of a complex representation given the contents of its constituents and its "structure." Locke is therefore committed to a language of thought for the building up of these complex representations. Of course he supplies

no such thing, but there are gestures towards it.

Later empiricists (e.g. Hume) deplored this kind of extension on the grounds that it allows for concepts, and hence judgments, where there is, by their lights, no possibility of justified belief.

4. Fodor (1987) attempts to avoid idealizations. His approach will be discussed in chapter 5.

5. Indeed, illusions are never the result of malfunction. If they were, they wouldn't be reliably producible between subjects. The case of illusion is doubly difficult for Locke, since his account allows for a cognitive state to have semantic properties only if that state is (or could be) a constituent of a percept. The CTC's accounts of the perceptual process invoke representations that show up only as constituents of "earlier" representations, never as constituents of percepts. See, e.g., Marr 1982. This problem can, perhaps, be solved by reformulating the definition in some such way as this: x represents y in LOCKE $=_{df}$ were LOCKE functioning properly, x would occur in an intermediate or final output of the perceptual system when, only when, and because LOCKE is confronted by y. There is an analogous extension in Fodor's (1987) treatment.

6. Appealing to idealization of this sort makes the Lockean account of representation explicitly epistemological. This will not be welcome news to those epistemologists who hope to help themselves to the notion of representation on the assumption that it can be regarded as an externally defined primitive.

Fodor (1987) attempts to argue that optimal conditions can be defined in a nonepistemological way, by reference to psychophysical conditions. More of this anon.

7. There is a temptation to say that the occurrence of P means something like this: *There is a 90% chance that a cat is present, and a 10% chance that there is a dog present.* But this can't be right, for it presupposes for its usefulness that the system has some way of representing dogs as opposed to cats, and this is just what is at issue.

8. Philosophers have been known to complain about this sort of use of the term "knowledge". I propose to avoid this sort of complaint by means of a cheap trick: I shall use the term "*knowledge" for what I mean. (Readers of Cummins 1983 will recognize this as a natural extension of a similar cheap trick used there.) *Knowledge consists of explicit representations whose propositional contents may or may not be true or justified but which are used by the system as if their propositional contents were both true and justified. (Actually, this requires a slight qualification: A system may use *knowledge with less than complete confidence. Perhaps it has a lot of *knowledge in a "useful conjectures" box or a "good enough for government work" box. Computationally, there is a difference between putting r in a box like that and putting "Maybe-r" in the gospel box. But our ability to make this sort of point shows how much better we understand *knowledge than knowledge, thanks to AI.)

9. It *should* go without saying by now that the reasoning in question is not the sort of thing codified in formal logic. See Harman 1987.

10. Pylyshyn (1984) is thus wrong to suggest, as he does, that psychologists

77777

working in the CTC tradition are, or should be, mainly interested in functional architecture.

11. This is the view expressed in Fodor 1987.

12. Sense data were supposed to be completely foolproof. What I am calling simple perceptual features here needn't be that insulated from reality; they need only (!) be infallibly detectable under ideal conditions without the use of any mediating *knowledge.

13. Locke's doctrine about the origin of concepts—that they are constructed by abstraction from experience—has the consequence, explicitly recognized, that no concept can specify a feature not specified perceptually (i.e., as ideas of sense or reflection). Locke's abstract ideas (LOCKE's master cards), and hence the beliefs etc. of which they are constituents, are severely limited in the contents they can encode. Locke didn't make much of it, but Hume and Ayer (1951) were prepared to condemn a lot to the flames on the strength of these restrictions. More recent wisdom takes these restrictions to be a knock on the doctrine rather than on the proscribed contents. If my argument is on the right track, contemporary "Lockean" accounts reinstate the same restrictions that undermined the plausibility of Locke's original version.

   Fodor, in a widely circulated 1985 manuscript called "Psychosemantics" (not to be confused with his book of that title), was aware of the verificationist core of the doctrine he espoused, but claimed that the doctrine had all the virtues (?) and none of the vices of traditional verificationism. I think it has all the vices. The virtues have always escaped me.

14. This is NOT the same as saying that the rigidity and continuity assumptions are "hardwired." Hardwiring *knowledge is just a special case of read-only memory: a representation that can't be altered computationally, though it might be altered in other ways (by a blow on the head, or a disease, say). Hardwired representations are representations and hence are not inexplicit.

15. Perhaps this isn't quite correct. Some inexplicit content derives from the form and medium of explicit data structures. I'm not sure whether to regard issues of form and medium as matters of architecture; *I think so*, but I'm not sure. But it doesn't really matter here; I can ignore these cases for the purposes of the present argument because they obviously presuppose explicit representation and hence cannot help to ground it.

16. For artificial systems, I suppose we have ideal *design* conditions. OK. Enough said.

Chapter 5

1. Recall that the Lockean theory identified representations with features of things that play a certain functional role: The covariance that mattered was covariance with the computationally operative features of percepts, *viz.*, punch patterns in percept cards. This was to rule out sun-to-sunburn correlations as cases of representation. Fodor is able to gloss over this detail by assuming from the start that we are talking about *symbols* in Mentalese. Sunburns, presumably, don't count. Ultimately, though, you need to say why they don't count, and the Lockean route seems the only one open to the covariationist.

Fodor does sometimes speak of stuffing | proton |s in the belief box, but this makes no sense, or the wrong sense. A | proton | doesn't express a belief. A | there are protons | does; however, that doesn't express a property, it expresses a proposition.

2. Fodor has, I think, different reasons for abandoning the idealization response to the disjunction problem. See Fodor 1987.

3. Fodor argues that there *are* observation terms in Mentalese, i.e., terms of Mentalese whose sufficient causal conditions can be specified by psychophysics, terms of Mentalese that express transducible properties (i.e., properties that, according to the CTC, can be reliably detected without *knowledge-driven inference). But these, as he freely admits, will not underwrite | proton |s, or even | cat |s, for what the observation terms of Mentalese express (assuming there are such things) are, at most, transducible properties. And, to repeat, if we know anything in philosophy, it is that we aren't going to be able to express a necessary and sufficient condition for being a cat in terms that represent transducible properties. What we need, instead, are properties like being a vertebrate mammal.

4. I have used my convention for naming Mentalese symbols where Fodor uses single quotes.

5. Because, if we can do that, then we don't have to say that all cats cause | cat |s; we can say, instead, that under conditions C all cats cause | cat |s. If under conditions C any cat would cause a | cat |, we needn't worry that | cat | really expresses the property of being a black-and-white cat, or that of being Graycat.

Chapter 6

1. The information that *t* is G is nested in the information that *s* is F just in case *s*'s being F carries the information that *t* is G.

2. See, for example, Fodor 1987 and the replies to Dretske 1983.

3. Dretske refers unlearned cases to evolution: The species (or whatever) does the learning, and the mechanism is natural selection. On the face of it, this seems quite hopeless, in view of the fact that natural selection will perpetuate features that are far from perfect indicators. The obvious cases are systems that save computation time, and Consequently the life of the organism, by generating a lot of false positives for predators. I am willing to bet that *nothing* in any individual or species was *ever* a perfect indicator of predator presence.

4. Perhaps Dretske's view is that *p* is the semantic content of *M* because that is the semantic content that tokens of *M* have in the learning condition. This, however, would allow for semantic contents in the absence of the corresponding informational contents, a result completely contrary to the spirit of Dretske's approach.

5. We will see eventually that Dretske in fact makes very little capital of the appeal to functions.

6. This isn't quite the same as assimilating misrepresentation to malfunction. The gauge doesn't malfunction when the tank is full of water (it isn't *broken*,

after all), but it does *fail to perform* its function of indicating the amount of fuel in the tank.

7. This was Fodor's suggestion in Fodor 1985. He has now abandoned it.

8. That Dretske does accept this constraint is evident from the fact that he is prepared to rule out the possibility that R means$_i$ that x obtains on the grounds that R doesn't covary with x, even under optimal conditions. See the quotation in the next section, where this point looms large.

   Millikan, as we will see in the next chapter, avoids this move by holding that something may have a function yet often (even typically) fail to perform it.

9. The same issues are addressed in Fodor 1985 and in Fodor 1984.

10. "Mean$_n$" is a synonym for "indicate" here.

11. Thus, I think it is fair to say that Dretske doesn't explain or make serious capital of the appeal to functions in M_f. He does, however, make serious capital of the difference between causation and covariance. As Millikan has pointed out to me, the direction of oxygen-free water isn't causally implicated in the behavior of the magnetosome at all!

Chapter 7

1. Perhaps this is a good place to emphasize again that the computational theory makes rather special demands on the concept of representation. Although we will find that Millikan's theory does not satisfy these demands, that does not, by itself, show that her theory is inadequate in other contexts, such as "folk psychology" or ethology.

2. I have changed Millikan's formulation somewhat in order to simplify the exposition. I don't believe any of the subsequent discussion is materially affected by the liberties I have taken.

3. The system in question may be an ecosystem, an organism, a cognitive system, or whatever the relevant context is for attributing Proper Functions.

4. This account applies straightforwardly to artifacts that have a history of replication: A Proper Function of aspirin tablets is to mitigate headache because it is their role in headache mitigation that is responsible for the fact that they continue to be manufactured. Artifacts with no history of replication have Proper Functions in virtue of their designers' intentions only.

5. This is my term, not Millikan's.

6. Millikan actually proceeds in terms of Normal Conditions (the conditions that must obtain if the item in question is to fulfill the function in question in accordance with a Normal Explanation). It seems preferable to avoid reference to explanation here, if possible, so as not to compromise the intended *naturalistic* character of the account. Millikan has confirmed in conversation that Normal Cases and *basic factors* fit the bill in this context.

7. Again, Millikan actually expresses this idea in terms of the minimal ("most proximal") Normal Explanation.

8. This discussion of basic factors is intended as friendly exposition. Juliette Zahedynour has convinced me that evolutionary theory will support no asymmetry between flower presence and predator absence that is compa-

rable to the asymmetry between pendulum length and friction that mechanics supports.

9. This is not, of course, the only Proper Function of the locomotion system.

10. Notice that Millikan, unlike Dretske, actually has a theory of functions to draw on, and hence the appeal to functions in the case of the magnetotaxic bacteria can do some work in arbitrating the liberal-conservative debate about the meaning of magnetosome orientation.

11. The merit is purely instrumental. Engaging in "selection history fantasy" is a useful way to think about function and design; it helps us understand why and how a system works now in the current environment. In this respect it is similar to Dennett's "intentional systems theory," which bids us think of a system in terms of a belief-desire structure guided by a perfect but realistic rationality (i.e., a rationality that takes resource constraints and constancies in the environment seriously).

12. Here is a possible history for the magnetotaxic bacteria: A large number of organisms—indeed the majority—swim toward the surface to their deaths, with the result that certain predators that naturally hang out near the surface are well fed and hence not tempted to go deeper, and this ensures the survival of the species of bacteria in question.

   The basic factors in the Normal Case are a little difficult to discern on this scenario, but it looks just possible that the magnetosomes might wind up meaning something like "predators to divert in the o-direction".

13. To avoid ambiguity over this possibility, Millikan's own example invokes a duplicate that is a cosmic accident.

14. It seems to me we always make a comparable assumption about a system when we think of it as a dynamical system: Its future path through phase space depends on its current state, never on how it got into that state (i.e., the actual historical path to that state).

Chapter 8

1. Functions associate values with arguments. To see a device as satisfying a function, therefore, is to see it as having inputs and outputs—starting and ending configurations, perhaps—and to see these as *arguments* and *values*, respectively. This suggests the following:

   d satisfies $g =_{df} g(x) = y$ iff, were x to occur in d, then, normally, y would occur in d.

   As it stands, this is not adequate. It will fail when f is many-one, i.e., when there is more than one way to get a given output; we need to specify that y is x's output and not, say, z's. Unfortunately, there is no general way to say what it is for y to be x's output for arbitrary d, y, and x. We have to do it case by case. In calculators, the output is typically the first stable display after input, i.e., the first display after input such that no other display occurs until another input occurs. But this definition won't generalize, nor will any other. We must, then, suppose that, for a given device d and function g, we can specify an input-output criterion—a criterion that allows us to say of a given state in d whether it is a value and, if so, which state of d is its input. The first stable output after input criterion lately mentioned is the standard input/ output criterion for calculators. Let us write $a_d \Longrightarrow v_d$ and mean "Were a to occur in d, then, normally, v would occur in d *as a's output.* " Then

d satisfies $g =_{df}$ there is an input/output criterion d and g such that $a_d \Longrightarrow v_d$ iff $g(a) = v$.

2. Of course, adding machines don't have to have buttons or displays. Any set of events or states will do so long as I/O behavior turns out to be addition under interpretation, i.e., so long as it is possible to treat those states or events as representations of addends and their sums.

3. Viewers of "It's the Easter Beagle, Charlie Brown!" will recognize that not everyone knows how to satisfy even this simple function.

    To some it sounds odd to say that hollandaise is *computed*, but it is essential to see that a fundamental insight of the theory of computation is that the objects of computation are precisely *arbitrary objects*. With our attention riveted on computational theories of cognition, we tend to think exclusively of the symbolic case—the case in which it is symbols (representations) that are computed. But, notoriously, the symbolic status of the objects of computation is irrelevant to the computation itself; what matters to the computation is just that the objects of computation can be reliably typed. See Haugeland 1981.

4. This definition might seem wrong, given that in a program one often has many calls to the same function; what determines which call is executed first? Well, the program counter keeps track of the flow of control. So, simply think of each function having a hidden argument—MYTURN—which is the state of control (a physical state of the system, of course) that must obtain for the function to be called.

5. It is easy to think of LISP or OPS5 programs in this way, as well as PASCAL. PROLOG and SMALLTALK are a little trickier because the functional structure is rather more implicit.

    When thinking about general-purpose computing systems, you must be careful to distinguish three different ways such systems execute programs: (i) A program may be stored as a data structure for an interpreter. (An interpreter is a program that accesses other programs and executes them.) Here, the program defines a virtual machine which is equivalent to a machine that (ii) simply has that program hardwired in the way that an addition program is hardwired in an adding machine. In the first case, the program defines the functional architecture (Pylyshyn 1984) of a virtual machine; in the second case, it defines a nonvirtual functional architecture. (iii) A program (usually called a rule in this context) may be stored as a data structure and accessed by a program that simply uses the rule to solve some problem or accomplish some task, as when one recalls and uses the program for taking square roots.

    The functional architecture of a computing system is a program in the sense defined in the text. That is, it is a set of inter-locking functions satisfied by the system. Pylyshyn often makes it sound as if the primitive operations of a programming language define a functional architecture, but this cannot be right. The functional architecture of the mind is supposed to be that aspect of the mind's structure that remains fixed across changes in data structures (i.e., in what is represented). This is the program (sense ii) itself, including its control structure, not the primitive operations of a language we might write it in.

6. I take this formulation from Darek Parfitt (1984), who argues that there is no "further fact" to personal identity beyond the facts of inter-psychological state relations.

7. By mechanical variables, here, I mean real mechanical properties that vary in magnitude. I do NOT mean symbols.

8. The tracking referred to here is not causal, of course. A computational system can simulate a natural one without there being any significant causal relations between a symbol and the property it tracks in the simulated system. This is important because it allows for the fact that a computational system can simulate hypothetical systems and counterfactual systems, as well as abstract systems and systems that are actual and concrete but not in any significant causal interaction with the similator.

9. As I use these terms, instantiation is a special case of simulation, viz., the case in which the interpretations are abstract objects of some kind: numbers, sets, propositions, concepts (construed not as psychological items but as corresponding to predicates in the way propositions correspond to sentences), truth conditions, and the like. I restrict instantiation to abstract functions (functions with abstracta as arguments and values) because instantiation seems most natural as a relation between something abstract and an instance. Simulation is just like instantiation except that the arguments and values of the function simulated needn't be abstracta.

10. For those who like definitions: r s-represents x in $S =_{df}$ there are functions f, g, and I such that S satisfies g, g simulates f under interpretation I, and $I(r) = x$.

11. Here we are talking not about a particular distance (3 meters, say) but about *whatever* distance an unaccelerated body travels for an arbitrarily specified velocity and time. Plug a velocity and a time into the geometry as the base and the height of the rectangle, respectively, and the volume is the distance traveled.

12. A "buggy" bridge program may *have* no Proper Interpretation in the bridge domain, if it is buggy enough. It might, by coincidence, have a Proper Interpretation in some other domain—a domain no one has thought of. In such a case, we have representation without realizing it, but not the representation we intended.

13. Indeed, this is something of a false dichotomy, since a data structure is what it is to some extent because of the processes that operate on it. The difference between a representation of a list and a set, after all, is typically simply a matter of whether it is possible to exploit order. We think of the fundamental data structures in LISP as lists because (car 'list) returns the *first* member of a list rather than some element or other (e.g., the one that *happens* to be first *on this particular occasion*).

14. Correction involves getting it right after all, perhaps by adding a special-case rule. Avoiding the error involves refusing to deal with cases in which failure is likely or inevitable.

15. Actually, I'm not at all sure about this. On the one hand, what makes an adding machine usable for us isn't what makes an adding machine. On the other hand, the question of explaining addition (or building an adding machine) comes up only in the context of some antecedently specified interpretation scheme—a scheme we know to be "workable" (i.e., usable by the systems that will need to use it).

16. In the mathematical cases it cannot be causal connections between symbol and number, because numbers have no causal powers.

17. It is sometimes important that a system can simulate a non-numerical function f while instantiating a numerical function f'. If we know what it is (i.e., if we can give it a standard mathematical expression), the numerical function f' will give us a mathematical handle on the instantiating function g, and hence (indirectly) a handle on f.

18. Actions are said to be rational or irrational, of course, but only because they are themselves Intentional (as well as, sometimes, intentional). Actions, as Aristotle pointed out, are assessable as rational just to the extent that they can be treated as *conclusions* (of practical syllogisms, say) and, hence, as having propositional contents. Mere behaviors—mere motions, Aristotle would have called them—cannot be so assessed. Actions are what Dretske (1981) would call digitized behaviors.

19. Part of the difficulty in reconciling covariance theories with the CTC is that they take the empiricist view that perception is the paradigm of cognition. But perception, as the empiricists conceived it, is not an inferential process, and hence there is no room for a CTC explanation of perception as empiricists conceived it. The CTC, of course, treats perception as an inferential process. This provides the CTC with an explanandum—a target function to simulate—and hence with some space for s-representation to play an explanatory role. But a corollary of this approach is that the distal object to percept relation is mediated by representation, and hence cannot be invoked to define the representation relation.

20. I mean here inference in the sense of Harman 1987, not inference in the sense of deductive proof.

    Systems of formal logic contain what are called rules of inference. But such rules don't tell you what to infer; they are only part of a system that determines the validity, not rationality, of an inference already made. They thus have little to do with inference as it is meant here, i.e., with inference construed as the essence of cognition: *generating* a result that is *rational* (rational enough) relative to the situation you are in.

21. The specification of a cognitive function is what Marr (1982) calls (somewhat misleadingly) giving a computational theory.

22. There is another possibility: that cognitive systems don't deal with clothing and faces "in their own terms"; they deal with such matters such as physics and chemistry deal with them. My suspicion is that this is not plausible on empirical grounds; for example, the psychological evidence that faces con-

stitute a "special" domain for people seems quite strong. See, e.g., Gregory 1970.

Chapter 9

1. Block's argument assumes that a two-factor theory will understand the external factor in a functional-role manner, and there is no reason why a two-factor theorist *must* do this. Perhaps what hooks internal functional roles to the world is not a network of causal or computational relations.
2. And not all of these; only the causal consequences that alter a state enough to alter its computational consequences will count. All the noise that doesn't matter, for example, doesn't count.
3. It is seldom noticed that the possibility of alternative causal realizations of the same computational system commits the CTC to the viability of a "narrow" conception of content and cognition just as much as the possibility of alternative environmental/historical embeddings of the same computational system.
    We really have several wide-narrow distinctions here: (i) Content determined by factors "in the head" (if there is any) is narrow relative to content determined by external factors. (ii) Content determined by computational factors (if there is any) is narrow relative to content determined by causal factors. (iii) Content determined by purely cognitive factors (if there is any) is narrow relative to content determined by noncognitive factors. (iv) Content determined by synchronic factors (present dispositions of whatever kind) is narrow relative to content determined by historical factors (e.g., selection history—see Millikan 1984). I am pretty sure all these distinctions are orthogonal to each other. Only the first distinction is typically noticed, because the popular arguments for wide determination are arguments for determination by factors "outside the head" (what Burge 1979 calls non-individualistic factors). Distinction iv should get some attention now that Millikan has argued that historical factors can determine content.
4. Perhaps calculators could be counted as simple cognitive systems, in which case their representational states would be of a piece with cognitive representation generally. I confess (blushingly) that I was once attracted by this position myself (see Cummins 1983). Another possibility would be to hold that calculators count as representational systems only because of the cognitive roles they have in virtue of interaction with genuine cognitive systems. Neither of these options is consistent with the perspective of the CTC.
5. The LISP print function, for example, returns a value (typically nil) which is seldom used (though it can be, and sometimes is). Actually, in LISP, printing is technically the side effect of executing a function that returns a value (true of nil). But typically it is the printing one cares about, not the returned value.
6. "At the wrong address": What I have in mind here is the sort of thing that happens in an assembly-language program when the system attempts to read as an instruction something the programmer intended as data, or *vice versa*. "Buggy access": It is appallingly easy to write code that sometimes

fails to properly read from or write to a complex data structure such as a frame or script. From the viewpoint of intended or optimal design, these are bugs, hence one kind of malfunction. But (alas) they do have genuine computational consequences that contribute their bit to making the system what it is. There seems no principled way to rule out such consequences; surely we cannot assume that the brain has no bugs.

7. The interpretationist approach bears an important resemblance to Paul Churchland's (1979) suggestion that the propositional attitudes link mental states to propositions in order to track the logical properties of the former in much the way that measurement links numbers to magnitudes in order to track the mathematical properties of the latter.

Chapter 10

1. Depending on one's philosophy of mathematics, it need not even imply that the relevant interpretation is constructable, or even that its existence is discoverable by some specified finite means.

2. The nonintentional status of the interpretationist explication of s-representation is, of course, conditional on the possibility of providing a nonintentional explication of the troublesome concept of direct interpretation. I can only repeat my faith in the transcendental argument of chapter 8: The CTC is surely right about adding machines, and right in a way that would explain adding in a machine that occurred quite by accident—say, as the unanticipated and unrecognized result of an incompetent attempt to design a mousetrap.

3. See Leeds 1986 for a persuasive defense of the claim that even the Received View overestimates the role that causation can plausibly be expected to play.

4. See chapters I and II of Cummins 1983 for a defense of the claim that scientific explanation is seldom causal explanation in any straightforward sense.

5. We should reject out of hand the idea that the cause specified might *be* a content: contents, I suppose, are such things as propositions, and these are certainly not individual causes (though having such-and-such content might be a causal factor).

6. Those who accept the Received View typically consider only causal statements involving propositional attitudes (e.g., "Her desire to avoid a scene led her to apologize") in their discussions of content causation. It is likely that the Received View is correct in supposing that the causal statements of so-called folk psychology don't generalize. But these are not the central cases of content ascription in the CTC. The central case—indeed the only case — for the CTC is ascription of content to a data structure.

7. This is what I called the *specification problem* in Cummins 1983 and in chapter 8 above.

8. See Haugeland 1978 for the important but much neglected distinction between analysis on different levels and analyses on different dimensions.

9. Interpretational semantics will have my data structures representing neither: If I could track *mice*, I could tell mice from shrews. Since I can't tell them apart, I can't track them, so no data structure in me is a genuine I mouse I or

a genuine |shrew|. So here is another way in which representational content fails to mirror intentional content (assuming, of course, that I can think about mice even though I can't tell them from shrews—an assumption that could surely be contested). If you are inclined to think that my inability to tell them apart means that I can't think about mice as opposed to shrews, you are free to return to the numerical examples. But then even covariance and adaptational role together won't help, because numbers don't have causal powers or selection histories.

10. Individualistic psychology (the term is from Burge 1979) is thus psychology that is narrow with respect to environment. The CTC also envisages a psychology that is narrow with respect to the mush or junk that realizes the computational architecture, and with respect to the selection history of that architecture. See note 4 to chapter 9 above.

Chapter 11

1. This chapter owes a great deal to Schwarz 1987. The present discussion grew out of a collaboration for a joint paper published as Cummins and Schwarz 1988.

2. A back-propagation process is simply a process that *begins* with a specification of the activation levels of the *output* nodes—typically a specification of the "correct output" for the previous input—and alters the connection strengths according to some rule.

3. This will be questioned shortly.

4. Individual nodes in distributed representation schemes are sometimes said to represent "micro-features," i.e., features that "add up to" (the "adding" depending on the representation scheme in use) a recognizable feature. The essential point is that the individual nodes of a distributed representation do not constitute an analysis, in any intuitive sense, of the feature represented by the pattern as a whole. Moreover, slightly different patterns may be construed as variant representations of the "same thing."

   For a careful but concise introduction to connectionism, see Smolensky (forthcoming).

5. Of course, not *all* of the data structures in the system need have elements of a cognitive function as interpretations. Typically, one supposes that the basic functions making up the functional architecture—functions satisfied by the system—often manipulate representations that have interpretations whose cognitive significance is indirect, i.e., interpretations that are cognitively significant only in virtue of the roles that play in the construction of symbols whose interpretations are governed by the target epistemological constraints.

6. Let us not underestimate the vast difference between the conservative connectionist and the proponent of the CTC. I simply want to point to one important point of agreement, namely that they share the same abstract conception of the problem of cognition and of the proper general strategy for attacking it.

7. Occasionalism suggests itself: God intervenes to guarantee the right symbols at the right times.

8. It isn't even necessary that these be *computed*. Though the relevant functions are certainly computed in the standard digital simulations, they might simply be *satisfied* in special-purpose hardware.
9. In Cummins and Schwarz 1988 we were overly conservative on this point, leaving it open that an algorithm defined at the single-node level might not "aggregate up" into an algorithm defined at the vector level. But it is obvious that the aggregation is always possible—indeed trivial.

Bibliography

Anderson, J. 1983. *The Architecture of Cognition*. Hillsdale, N.J.: Erlbaum.

Ayer, A.J. 1951. *Language, Truth and Logic*. Second edition (first published in 1936). New York: Dover.

Bealer, G. 1984, "Mind and Anti-Mind: Why Thinking Has No Functional Definition." *Midwest Studies in Philosophy* 9:283-328.

Bennett, J. 1971. *Locke, Berkeley, Hume: Central Themes*. Oxford University Press.

Bennett, J. 1976. *Linguistic Behavior*. Cambridge University Press.

Block, N. 1978. "Troubles with Functionalism." In *Minnesota Studies in the Philosophy of Science, volume 9, Perception and Cognition: Issues in the Foundations of Psychology*, ed. C.W. Savage. Minneapolis: University of Minnesota Press.

Block, N. 1986. "Advertisement for a Semantics for Psychology." *Midwest Studies in Philosophy* 10: 615-678.

Block, N. 1987. "Functional Role and Truth Conditions." *Proceedings of the Aristotelian Society* suppl. 61: 157–181.

Burge, T. 1979. "Individualism and Psychology." *Philosophical Review* 95: 3-45.

Churchland, Paul. 1979. *Scientific Realism and the Plasticity of Mind*. Cambridge University Press.

Churchland, Patricia. 1986. *Neurophilosophy*. Cambridge, Mass: MIT Press. A Bradford Book.

Cummins, R. 1975a. "Functional Analysis." *Journal of Philosophy* 72: 741-760.

Cummins, R. 1975b. "The Philosophical Problem of Truth-of." *Canadian Journal of Philosophy* 5: 103-122.

Cummins, R. 1979. "Intention, Meaning and Truth Conditions." *Philosophical Studies* 35: 345-360.

Cummins, R. 1982. "PATHFINDER: Investigating the Acquisition of Communicative Conventions." In *Proceedings of the Cognitive Science Society*.

Cummins, R. 1983. *The Nature of Psychological Explanation*. Cambridge, Mass.: MIT Press. A Bradford Book.

Cummins, R. 1986. "Inexplicit Information." In *The Representation of Knowledge and Belief*, ed., M. Brand and R.M. Harnish. Tucson: University of Arizona Press.

Cummins, R.   1987.   "Why Adding Machines Are Better Examples   than Thermostats: Comments on Dretske's 'The explanatory role of content.' " In *Contents of Thought: Proceedings of the 1985 Oberlin Colloquium in Philosophy*. Tucson: University of Arizona Press.

Cummins, R., and G. Schwarz. 1988. "Prospects for a Radical Connectionism." *Southern Journal of Philosophy 26 (Supplement, Spindel Conference, 1987: Connectionism and the Philosophy of Mind)*: 43-62.

Davidson, D.   1975.   "Thought and Talk."   In *Mind and Language*, ed. S. Guttenplan. Oxford University Press.

Dennett, D.   1978.   *Brainstorms*. Cambridge, Mass.: MIT Press. A Bradford Book.

Dennett, D.   1987.   The Intentional Stance. Cambridge, Mass.: MIT Press.   A Bradford Book.

Dretske, F.   1981.   Knowledge and the Flow of Information. Cambridge, Mass.: MIT Press. A Bradford Book.

Dretske, F. 1983. "Precis of Knowledge and the Flow of Information." *Behavioral and Brain Sciences* 6, no. 1: 55-63.

Dretske, F.   1986.   "Misrepresentation."   In *Belief*, ed. R. Bodgan. Oxford University Press.

Dretske, F. 1987. "The explanatory role of content." In *Contents of Thought: Proceedings of the 1985 Oberlin Colloquium in Philosophy*. Tucson: University of Arizona Press.

Dretske, F. 1988. *Explaining Behavior*. Cambridge, Mass.: MIT Press. A Bradford Book.

Dreyfus, H., and S. Dreyfus. 1985. *Mind Over Machine*. New York: Free Press.

Field, H. 1971. "Tarski's Theory of Truth." *Journal of Philosophy* 69: 347-375.

Field, H. 1977. "Logic, Meaning and Conceptual Role." *Journal of Philosophy* 74: 379-409.

Field, H. 1978. "Mental Representation." *Erkentniss* 13: 9-61.

Fodor, J. 1975. *The Language of Thought*. New York: Crowell.

Fodor, J. 1981. *Representations*. Cambridge, Mass.: MIT Press. A Bradford Book.

Fodor, J.   1983.   *The Modularity of Mind*. Cambridge, Mass.: MIT Press.   A Bradford Book.

Fodor, J.   1984a.   "Why Paramecia Don't Have Mental   Representations." *Midwest Studies in Philosophy* 10: 3-23.

Fodor, J. 1984b. "Semantics Wisconsin Style." *Synthese* 59: 231- 50.

Fodor, J. 1985. Psychosemantics. Unpublished manuscript.

Fodor, J. 1987. *Psychosemantics*. Cambridge, Mass.: MIT Press. A Bradford Book

Gregory, R. 1970. *The Intelligent Eye*. New York: McGraw-Hill.

Grice, H. P. 1957. "Meaning." *Philosophical Review* 66: 377-388.

Grice, H. P. 1968. "Utter's Meaning, Sentence-Meaning, and Word- Meaning." *Foundations of Language* 4: 225-242.

Grice, H. P. 1969. "Utter's Meaning and Intentions." *Philosophical Review* 78: 147-177.

Harman, G. 1982. "Conceptual Role Semantics." *Notre Dame Journal of Formal Logic* 23: 242-256.

Harman, G. 1987. *Change in View*. Cambridge, Mass.: MIT Press. A Bradford Book.

Haugeland, J. 1978. "The Nature and Plausibility of Cognitivism." *Behavioral and Brain Sciences* 2: 215-260.

Haugeland, J. 1981. "Semantic Engines." In *Mind Design*, ed. J. Haugeland. Cambridge, Mass.: MIT Press, 1981. A Bradford Book.

Haugeland, J. 1985. *Artificial Intelligence: The Very Idea.* Cambridge, Mass.: MIT Press. A Bradford Book.

Leeds, S. 1982. Causation and the Mental. Unpublished manuscript.

Lewis, D. 1969. *Convention.* Cambridge, Mass.: Harvard University Press.

Loar, B. 1982. "Conceptual Role and Truth Conditions." *Notre Dame Journal of Formal Logic* 23: 272-283.

Loar, B. 1985. "Social Content and Psychological Content." In *Contents of Thought: Proceedings of the 1985 Oberlin Colloquium in Philosophy.* Tucson: University of Arizona Press.

Lycan, W. 1981. "Form, Function and Feel." *Journal of Philosophy* 78: 24-49.

Lycan, W. 1987. *Consciousness.* Cambridge, Mass.: MIT Press. A Bradford Book.

Marr, D. 1982. *Vision.* New York: Freeman.

McGinn, C. 1982. "The Structure of Content." In *Thought and Content*, ed. A. Woodfield. Oxford University Press.

Millikan, R. 1984. *Language, Thought and Other Biological Categories.* Cambridge, Mass.: MIT Press. A Bradford Book.

Millikan, R. 1986. "Thoughts Without Laws: Cognitive Science Without Content." *Philosophical Review* 95: 47-80.

Papineau, D. 1985. "Representation and Explanation." *Philosophy of Science* 51: 550-572.

Parfitt, D. 1984. *Reasons and Persons.* Oxford University Press.

Pollock, J. 1987a. *Contemporary Theories of Knowledge.* Totowa, N.J.: Rowman and Littlefield.

Pollock, J. 1987b. "How to Build a Person." *Philosophical Perspectives* 1: 109–154.

Putnam, H. 1975. "The Meaning of Meaning." In *Language, Mind and Knowledge*, ed. K. Gunderson. Minneapolis: University of Minnesota Press.

Putnam, H. 1983. "Computational Psychology and Interpretation Theory." In *Realism and Reason*, volume 3 of Philosophical Papers. Cambridge University Press.

Pylyshyn, Z. 1984. *Computation and Cognition.* Cambridge, Mass.: MIT Press. A Bradford Book.

Quine, W. V. O. 1960. *Word and Object.* Cambridge, Mass.: MIT Press.

Rumelhart, D., and J. McClelland. 1982. "An interactive activation model of context effects in letter perception: Part 2. The contextual enhancement of effect and some tests and extension of the model." *Psychology Review* 89: 60-94.

Rumelhart, D., J. McClelland, and the PDP Research Group. 1986. *Parallel Distributed Processing* (two volumes). Cambridge, Mass.: MIT Press. A Bradford Book.

Schiffer, S. 1981. "Truth and the Theory of Content." In *Meaning and Understanding*, ed. H. Parret and J. Bouraresse. Berlin: Walter de Gruyter.

Schiffer, S. 1982. "Intention Based Semantics." *Notre Dame Journal of Formal Logic* 23: 119-159.

Schwarz, G. 1987. Explaining Cognition as Computation. Master's Thesis, University of Colorado.

Searle, J. 1983. *Intentionality*. Cambridge University Press.

Smolensky, P. 1988. "The Proper Treatment of Connectionism." *Behavioral and Brain Sciences* 11, no. 1: 1–74.

Smolensky, P. Forthcoming. *Lectures on Connectionist Modeling*. Hillsdale, N.J. Erlbaum.

Stalnaker, R. 1984. *Inquiry*. Cambridge, Mass.: MIT Press. A Bradford Book.

Stich, S. 1983. *From Folk Psychology to Cognitive Science*. Cambridge, Mass.: MIT Press. A Bradford Book.

Tarski, A. 1956. "The Concept of Truth in Formalized Languages." In *Logic, Semantics and Metamathematics*, ed. A. Tarski. Oxford University Press.

Turing, A. 1950. "Computing Machinery and Intelligence." *Mind* 59: 434-460.

Ullman, S. 1979. *The Interpretation of Visual Motion*. Cambridge, Mass.: MIT Press.

Name Index

Subject Index